DO NOT
TWEET
AT AN IEP MEETING

ANNE I. TREIMANIS, ESQ.

...AND OTHER TIPS AND

STRATEGIES TO NEGOTIATE

SPECIAL EDUCATION SERVICES

Ranks Publishing, Inc.

Do Not Tweet at an IEP Meeting

...and other tips and strategies to negotiate special education services

Anne I. Treimanis, Esq.

COPYRIGHT AND PUBLISHER INFORMATION

Kiera Publishing, Inc. publication © 2016, Kiera Publishing, Inc.

https://www.facebook.com/kiera.publishing

All Rights Reserved.

Cover designed by Aria Rastandeh. http://aria.portfoliobox.me

ISBN: 978-0-9981875-0-1

CONTENTS

 Attorney Anne I. Treimanis limits her practice to special education, civil rights, and LGBTQ issues. You can read more about her practice at http://spedlawyers.com. Attorney Treimanis is also a popular presenter on disability issues at local, state-wide, national, and even several international conferences. She is also an adjunct professor at Saint Joseph University, teaching graduate classes on Special Education Law. Attorney Treimanis is the founder and Executive Director of SPED*NET, Special Education Network of New Canaan, Ltd. Attorney Treimanis graduated from Hofstra University School of Law. She is admitted to the NY, NJ, and CT bars, and most recently admitted to the bar of the United States Supreme Court.

Prior to running a law practice, Anne was a social worker, working to get adults with disabilities successfully situated in the community during the era of closing institutions. She was privileged to work closely with various ARC organizations.

Anne is the mother of four children. Her daughter Ieva has Down syndrome and was fully and successfully included at New Canaan Public Schools in New Canaan, CT. Yep, Ieva even took Algebra!

Being a Warrior for Special Education Matters

Attorney Nora Belanger

It is my great pleasure to write a Foreword to the book <u>Do Not Tweet at an IEP Meeting,</u> by Attorney Anne Treimanis.

First, it is my pleasure because of my long-time friendship and twenty year professional collaboration with Attorney Treimanis in the practice of special education and disability rights law. Together we refined our skills in enforcing the federal law called the Individuals with Disabilities Education Act (the IDEA). The IDEA allows students with disabilities to access a Free and Appropriate Public Education (FAPE), similar to what any student would receive. The cornerstone of FAPE is the Individualized Education Plan (IEP); the document which provides the specific elements of the individualized program developed for the student at the IEP meeting. To attorneys who represent parents on behalf of their children in this area of law; it is a matter of civil rights. It dictates that your child with autism, or dyslexia, or ADHD, or mental illness (to name a few disabilities) has the right to an appropriate education which allows him or her to make reasonable progress academically, socially and emotionally and to transition to post-secondary employment, post-secondary education and independent living.

Second, it is my pleasure to write the forward because the single most critical predictor of success in reaching your goal for your child with a disability is knowledge of your rights. The very purpose of the law is to insure FAPE; but also to allow parents to be an equal participant in the process of educating their child. Navigating the process is both complicated and bureaucratic. I predict that no one in your child's school will approach you with specific information about how to enhance your child's educational program, or to make you aware of your rights as a parent. They will not encourage you to insist on a research-based reading program when your child is years behind grade level, or suggest additional behavioral consulting in the school for your child with behavioral issues. You will need to educate yourself on the disability and on your rights under the law. You can do this by reading on the subject, by attending presentations, and by hiring evaluators, advocates and attorneys who will help lead you through the process. The school district is not incentivized to promote awareness of the process or of your rights for two important reasons: budget and precedent.

Do Not Tweet at an IEP Meeting is designed to educate parents and those whose mission is to assist students with disabilities. This is a complex area of law, which is fact-specific and fraught with political tactics and strategies. This book allows parents to even the playing field with schools, who are "repeat players" in that they are represented by attorneys on a continual basis for hundreds of students. It will encourage parents to learn what their child may need, what they can reasonably ask of the school and what the requirements are for schools to identify their child and educate students from age three through transition to adulthood. You will need to learn how to advocate for your child; whether it is by asking for evaluations, requesting modifications and accommodations, accessing specific services or hiring consultants with expertise to address the student's needs.

Remember that students with disabilities are among the most vulnerable in our society. An appropriate education can create a profound difference in the course of their future by promoting not just academic success, but independence and active participation in the workforce. Be sure to chart progress, seek your own experts and challenge the school district. Surround yourself with parents and other like-minded individuals who understand that educational rights apply to every child. The key to success is to educate yourself on your legal rights, to advocate as early as possible and to insert yourself as an equal participant on your child's educational team. Demand respect of school team members, establish credibility, and most of all, never, ever, give up! Your child with a disability is entitled to an individualized program to fit his or her educational needs. Attorney Treimanis has the background and the expertise to help you navigate the process and inspire you to reach your child's educational goals!

About Attorney Nora Belanger:

Nora Belanger, Esq. is a special education and disability rights attorney in Norwalk, Connecticut. She has been in practice for over fourteen years and has successfully represented hundreds of children with disabilities. Having been a special education teacher in a prior career, Attorney Belanger brings this experience to her legal practice. Attorney Belanger has been a speaker at numerous parent groups on the subject of special education law and parent's rights.

Attorney Belanger received a Juris Doctor from Pace University School of Law where she graduated with honors and served as Executive Editor of the Pace Law Review. She published an article in the Pace Law Review in the Fall of 2000 called "The ADA-A Practitioner's Guide in the Aftermath of Sutton: Sutton v. United Air Lines.". Attorney Belanger also has an MBA from the University of Connecticut where she graduated with honors and a B.S. in Special Education.

Meet Nora at http://norabelangerlaw.com.

My entire personal and professional life has been dedicated to advocating for individuals with disabilities. I want to make a positive difference. But I am unable to personally assist every family. This book is my attempt to share the best of what I know, so all families can be empowered with the information they need to help their child.

Enjoy these tips. I welcome every reader to share their best tips with me. If I use your tips in the next edition of this book, you will be credited in the List of Contributors. Email your tips to do.not.tweet.tips@gmail.com.

Anne

ACKNOWLEDGEMENTS AND DEDICATIONS

This book is dedicated first and foremost to my daughter Ieva, whose very existence defines my professional endeavors. I also dedicate this book to my three boys, Robbie, Karl, and Erik, each of whom are fierce disability advocates. Thanks for your support and for holding on to each other. Our journey has had some unexpected turns.

I want to share my deep appreciation to the family I was born into, the unforgettable Treimanis clan! They always believed in my dreams and supported me every step of my way.

Thanks to all the educators from New Canaan Public Schools in Connecticut. Because they rose to the occasion to successfully and fully include Ieva, my daughter had friends, became a proficient reader, and blossomed into a beautiful young adult. And as a side perk - I was permitted to have a life beyond micromanaging my daughter's education.

I wish to acknowledge SPED*NET, Special Education Network of New Canaan, Ltd, whose current board president is Judi Anders. This band of parents is committed to supporting all families in New Canaan who have children with disabilities. Parents can stand on the shoulders of those who came before them, to insure that their children get good programs. Thanks to all of the speakers who paraded in and out, every month for the past 15 years, to bring free informational programs to our community.

There are so many people to thank for making my life's work possible. I am currently surrounded by some extraordinary professionals in the office, Attorney Nora Belanger; Special

Education Advocates Gerri Fleming, Sonali Sarma, and Linda Talbert; Jane Ross from Smart Kids with LD, and my office manager Anita Budd. They are always available to discuss cases and share resources. Gerri Fleming, whose fierce advocacy and intelligence intimidates me, generously edited this book and also contributed many of the templates in this book. I have access to many professionals in the field, many of whom are so generous with their time. My work is made easier by the strong and cohesive network of special education attorneys and advocates in Connecticut who freely support and advise one another during our crusade for justice.

I thank each and every one of my clients in my private law practice. They trust me with their matters. I am privileged to walk along the road with them.

I thank the disability advocates who have inspired me. Some have mentored me. A special thank you to the late Robert Perske, Street-Court-Prison Worker & Author. He trusted me to collaborate on several projects together. He took me along to several events where I joyfully rode on his coattails.

I am inspired by all of the parents I know who stood up and took a leadership role in their community. In nearby Stamford, Connecticut, the legendary Robin Portanova started Stamford Education 4 Autism. They have raised tens of thousands of dollars to spend where needed, including giving out iPads to students with IEPs. She also started a pop-up store, *Just a Peace*, so students with disabilities could learn to work.

I thank the University of Saint Joseph in West Hartford for inviting me to teach graduate classes on Special Education Law. I learn so much from all of my students, each of whom is earning a Masters in Special Education, to be better prepared to teach the students that I happen to care about.

I thank the Surrogate Office at the Connecticut State Department of Education, who assigns students to me to assist in school matters. These are among the most vulnerable group of students, those who have been removed from their family of origin by the Department of Children and Families. I appreciate the opportunity to try to positively shape the school experience for these children. One of these students, Jackie, became my foster daughter. She positively influenced my family for the time we had together.

Finally, I am especially indebted to one of my closest colleagues and good friend, Dr. Kathleen Whitbread, who edited and contributed much of the material in this book. Dr. Whitbread co-authored my first book, IEP and Inclusion Tips for Parents and Teachers in 2006. That book was published by the Attainment Company, Inc. Many of those tips have found their way into this book. Dr. Whitbread has made Connecticut a better place to live, especially for individuals with intellectual disabilities.

TIPS FOR PREPARING FOR THE IEP

1. Find some uninterrupted time to spend with your child. Speak to him/her about what is happening at school. Ask him/her to list the top five best things about their classes. Then let him/her pretend h/she is king or queen for the day and ask what would be different. Allow them to "rate" their teachers or give them report cards. Ask him/her to tell you about all of the other students in the classroom or in the lunch room and playground. Does your child know the names of the other students at school? Talk about the kids on the bus. Listen carefully. If your child does not have traditional verbal skills, or is a poor reporter, request that you or a consultant conduct an observation at school. Volunteer in the classroom.

2. Get a full copy of your child's records prior to the meeting. You are entitled to one free copy in some states. Make this request every year. Don't just smile and pat the box when you get the records. Read them! If there is something inaccurate or inappropriate in the records, make sure you correct the records or ask that documents are expunged. If records are missing, then submit them to the school and ask that they are placed in the record. Get familiar with parent rights regarding records under IDEA (Individuals with Disabilities Education Act) and also FERPA (Family Education Rights and Privacy Act). See Appendix

1 for sample record request letter, also known as a FERPA Request.

3. Make a list of all of your concerns and your child's concerns. Submit these to the school in advance of the meeting and ask that the school attach your concerns to the IEP document. IDEA says that Parent and Student concerns must be considered when developing an IEP. One way to make sure you do not forget to list every concern is to read the FERPA file (student records) and highlight all deficits in one color, and all of the strengths in another color. See Appendix 2 for sample concerns document.

4. Special Education Advocate Gerri Fleming urges parents to pre-emptively include various concerns on the IEP that if acted upon might lead to suspension or worse. In this way, if the student gets in trouble for writing something highly inappropriate on Facebook regarding something that violates the school's code of conduct then you have your Parent Concerns to fall back on. This will assist you at the manifestation determination hearing. For example, list under parent concerns:

- At risk for exploitation by others, easily led - for the kid who follows and who may do something on a dare
- Does not know how to respond appropriately to others of the opposite sex - for the kid who desperately wants a girlfriend/boyfriend and may stalk or try something inappropriate

- Poor social skills/cognition-for the kid who has trouble with social problem solving in the moment
- Fails to comprehend the pitfalls of social media and the Internet—for the kid who may download porn or write something inappropriate in email, on Facebook or Twitter, etc...
- Understands the mechanics of sex, but not the wide-reaching implications of relationships and dealings with the opposite sex—for the kid who wants a relationship but may go about it in the wrong way
- Fails to read the signs of interest or disinterest by members of the opposite sex—for the kid who may be seen as stalking someone else
- Impulsive—for the kid who will act before thinking
- Easily frustrated—for the kid who is reactive

5. If you have information about your child that you wish to share with the school, prepare that information ahead of time. For example, if a doctor or specialist is treating your child, you may want them to provide a summary for the school if that information can be useful. You might also bring in samples of student work.

6. Maintain good records in connection with your child. Have a notebook with you at all times, and certainly one next to all phones. Immediately after each phone call, write down everything that was said, creating a "contemporaneous business record." If the conversation was important, follow up with a

letter or email confirming the conversation. See Appendix 3 for sample follow-up letter after a telephone conversation.

7. Before the IEP meeting, make sure you have a copy of all evaluations, together with proposed goals and objectives. Ask if there is a draft IEP and request a copy five days before the meeting. See Appendix 4 for sample letter requesting documents before the IEP meeting.

8. Make an appointment with each of your child's teachers and other professionals who interface with your child. Find out what they see as your child's strengths and needs. Your questions will help avoid surprises at the IEP meeting. Ask what h/she may need in order to be an effective teacher (or therapist or counselor). Ask the teacher, "what are your goals for my child in the upcoming year?" Use this meeting to resolve any concerns and get questions answered so the time you spend at the meeting can be as productive as possible.

9. If evaluations have been performed, meet with the evaluator to discuss the report ahead of time. Make sure you thoroughly understand the report. It might be helpful to Google the evaluation that was given so you have a fundamental understanding of the testing. Make sure all the subtests were administered; if they were not, ask why not.

10. If you have done private evaluations, share them with the school at least five days before the meeting so the school has time to review your reports. Remember that IDEA requires the IEP team to "consider" the evaluation; they are not required to

follow the recommendations. Be sure to pull all strengths and deficits revealed in private testing into your Parent Concerns document so as to make this testing part of the IEP record.

11. If you are thinking about outplacement or about other programs within the district, or if the school is thinking about it, ask for a visit to be arranged to this placement before the IEP meeting takes place.

12. Make sure you really understand your child's disability. Join organizations that can provide you with useful information. For example, if your child has Down syndrome, get active with one of the national organizations (National Down Syndrome Congress and National Down Syndrome Society) as well as your local or state chapters.

13. Visit your child's school and observe him/her across several settings. Try to do some volunteer work in the places that your child will be.

14. Get your child's records organized in a binder with tabs and a table of contents. Or you can keep them in files, labeled evaluations, IEPs, correspondence, report cards, etc.

15. Since every IEP document includes present levels of academic achievement and functional performance, be sure to have your ideas ready. Create a template from the form your state uses. Use the template to fill in what you see as your child's strengths, concerns, and the impact on the student's disability for involvement in the general curriculum (or

participation in appropriate preschool activities). See Appendix 5 for sample Present Levels template.

16. Read the Notice of the IEP – read all of it, don't just glance at the date. Check what is the purpose of the meeting and exactly who is invited. Are all of the critical players there? Is everyone who is legally supposed to be there invited? Think carefully before agreeing to excuse someone from attending. If you are planning to bring someone to the meeting, as a courtesy, let the school know. This is especially important if you plan to bring your attorney, because they may adjourn the meeting so they can get the school board attorney there. You can bring someone who has specialized knowledge of your child, or simply someone who will take notes and give you emotional support.

17. When you read the Notice of the IEP and check what is the purpose of the meeting, make sure that you understand and agree with the purpose of each meeting. Don't forget that the time set must be a mutually convenient time for the school and the family. Ask for an agenda, so you understand what will be covered at the meeting. If you have a topic you wish to discuss, let the school know. If you called the meeting, provide the school team with your agenda, and run the meeting like you are the chairperson.

18. Know what your legal rights are before you attend the meeting. Read IDEA. Become familiar with the information on your State Department of Education website, as well as the US Department of Education. Sign up for training on the law. Ask

for training at your IEP meeting. Get the IEP team to fund your training.

19. Network with other parents in your school district or those who have children with similar profiles. You will profit from these relationships. You will get to know what is going on in your schools.

20. The parents who are empowered with the most information seem to get the best programs for their kids.

TIPS ON SURVIVING THE IEP MEETING

1. Arrive at the meeting at least a few minutes early. Your cell phone ringer should be on silent. You'll have your files, together with a pen and pad of paper, unless you take your notes on an iPad. If the Student is present, make sure h/she has a pen and pad of paper in front of him/her as well. Sit at the head of the table and look poised and confident, ready to run the meeting. Your advocate and/or the team you have assembled should sit next to you.

2. Pay attention, do not check your text messages, and Do Not Tweet during an IEP meeting.

3. There may be different size chairs. The comfortable chairs that belong in the conference room and the metal uncomfortable folding chairs that were brought in to accommodate the extra people. Do not hesitate for you and your assembled team to sit in the comfortable chairs:

I was in an IEP meeting with one of my surrogate kids, who happened to be 19. Part of his disability was being oblivious to social conventions and he immediately jumped into a comfy overstuffed chair. The administrator was miffed, and he motioned to the student to move into a folding chair. I realized at that moment that chairs really do matter and that the administrator saw my child as a devalued member of the IEP team.   ~Anne Treimanis

4. Think about what you will wear. Choose clothing that is professional. Don't look like you are ready to work out at the YMCA or ready to work in the garden. Don't allow a power differential based on clothing.

5. You will have shared your written concerns ahead of time, but assume that no one will bring a copy. Have several copies available for the school and pass them out right away.

6. If you keep your files in a binder, put your child's photograph on the binder. It helps the team stay focused on why they are meeting.

7. Bring bottled and sparkling water and maybe some food. Don't take anything back with you; use disposable trays not your best dishes. If the staff is too uncomfortable to eat, don't worry, they will chow down later. Feel hopeful and festive. As Pennsylvania Advocate Colleen Tomko says, "You're not planning a funeral, you're planning for your child's success, make it fun." Author's note: Colleen also advocates for food, color and music. When I attend one of her festive IEP meetings, I'll report back on how that went!

8. Bring a Proposal Matrix to keep track of what you requested and how the school responded. These are your personal notes, do not share a copy with the school if they request them. See Appendix 6 for Proposal Matrix.

9. There seems to be predictable canned responses that school teams will say. Learn these lines and practice your answers. Here are some examples. See Appendix 7 for more examples:

Staff: "The team feels..."
Parent: "But I am a full member of the IEP team and I do not feel that way."
Staff: "We love your daughter."
Parent: "That's great, but she has all the love she needs. I love my daughter, my family loves her. I need you to teach her how to read."

10. See yourself as a full and equal member of the IEP team, on the same level as the professionals around the table. You may not be a highly qualified special educator, but you have known your child since 9 months before they were born. The school sees your child for 6 hours a day, 180 days a year, but you see them getting ready for school, after school, nights, weekends, sick days, holidays, and summers. You bring in the unique perspective that only a parent can have. Tell the school, "I am an expert on my child."

11. Be an active listener. Most people suck at listening. Active listening requires:

- Look at the person who is speaking. Do not slouch, sit up straight and lean slightly forward towards the speaker.

Do not jump across the table and lunge at the speaker if you are angry. If you do, the school might call the police and you will sit in jail instead of sitting at home eating dinner with your child.

- Maintain eye contact. Do not glare at the person.
- Do not check your Facebook page while they speak. There will be plenty of time to look at your Facebook page (or snoop on theirs!) after the meeting.
- Occasionally nod your head or say uh-huh. You may want to smile or laugh if appropriate. Never flirt with the person speaking.
- Do not have a side-bar conversation while someone is speaking. And do not allow a side-bar from the school team.
- Listen to what is being said instead of spending your time formulating what your response will be. You are not listening when you are busy preparing a rebuttal. Do not interrupt with counter arguments; it will leave the speaker frustrated and you will not hear what the speaker has to say.
- Keep an open mind; do not assume that the speaker has a hidden agenda (such as the school budget). That may be the case, but you can't know that, i.e. prove it. So leave that alone, for now.
- If you need clarification on what was said, then wait for them to finish speaking before you ask.
- Do not make disrespectful statements. Remain above-board at all times.

- NEVER put your arm in the air and say "Speak to the hand."

12. The law says that parents are full participants in the IEP process. If you did not receive the draft IEP ahead of time, or copies of any reports or evaluations, consider asking that the meeting be rescheduled. It's really difficult to listen to a report, try to understand it, respond to it, and then be prepared to use the information in creating an appropriate program. That is not meaningful participation! If you prepared properly for this meeting and advised the school that you needed the reports, evaluations, and draft IEP at least five days ahead of time, this scenario can be avoided. Don't feel uncomfortable to request that a meeting is rescheduled; consider it as part of staff training.

13. Think about inclusive education. Fully discuss any barriers your child may have in order to receive educational benefits in the general education environment. Do not assume that your child needs a more restrictive setting. Have a conversation about what supports and services your child needs to be successful.

14. When an evaluation is being presented, you must be prepared by having read the report and met with the evaluator. You will have prayed to Lord Google to give you a full understanding of all assessments used. If you disagree with the school's evaluation, you are entitled to an Independent Educational Evaluation (IEE) at the district's expense. Ask for

one at the IEP meeting and make sure that your request is noted in the IEP document. The school district is required to pay for the IEE unless the District plans to file for due process to prove that the school evaluation was appropriate. As with all facets of special education, make sure you are familiar with the laws surrounding the IEE. Often times a school district will provide the IEE, rather than file for due process. The IEE will interject some objectivity into the case.

15. Make sure you ALWAYS have a full size Bell Curve with you, laminated, so you can understand standard scores and test results. See Appendix 8 to look at a Bell Curve. It's also good to have a Psychometric Conversion Table handy. See Appendix 9.

16. Goals cannot be discussed until you have fully discussed the child's Present Level of Academic Achievement and Functional Performance. You cannot write goals until you understand who the child is, his/her strengths and needs, and the impact the disability has on accessing the general education curriculum. Present Levels of Academic Achievement and Functional Performance insures both for parent and student's input is considered. It means that evaluations, if needed, both formal and informal, are conducted and discussed.

17. When the team writes goals, make sure they are SMART, which means they are Specific, Measurable, Action oriented, Realistic, and Time measurable.

18. Be sure you understand the Prior Written Notice (PWN) page of your child's IEP. IDEA says that notice must be given whenever the school proposes to initiate a change or refuses to make a change in connection with: the identification, evaluation, or educational placement of the child, or the provision of FAPE to the child. This notice must include a description of the action proposed or refused by the agency; an explanation of why the agency proposes or refuses to take the action, a description of any other options that the agency considered and the reasons why those options were rejected; a description of each evaluation procedure, test, record, or report the agency used as a basis for the proposed or refused action; a description of any other factors that are relevant to the agency's proposal or refusal; a statement that the parents of a child with a disability have protection under the procedural safeguards of this part and, if this notice is not an initial referral for evaluation, the means by which a copy of a description of the procedural safeguards can be obtained; and sources for parents to contact to obtain assistance in understanding the provisions of this part. Insist on PWN for every significant proposal that you give the school that they either accept or reject. If you do not receive PWN, create your own and send it to the school. Ask that it be attached to the IEP.

19. Do not permit a discussion of placement until the present level of performance has been discussed, and then the goals and objectives. The law says that placement is discussed only after the IEP goals and objectives have been developed. When

you think about placement, remember that special education is a service, not a place.

20. Consider placement in general education for your child. A regular class placement, commonly called "inclusion," is defined by the Office of Special Education Programs (OSEP) as 80% or more of the day in a regular class. Don't be afraid to insist that this be considered. The law says that to the maximum extent appropriate, children with disabilities shall be educated in their neighborhood schools and attend regular classes (the classes h/she would have attended if born without a disability) with supplemental aids and services necessary for success. There is ample research to show that inclusion is good for all kids—with and without disabilities. Make the commitment and decide what supports are necessary to make it work. It is never too late to start.

21. If you don't understand what is being said, ask for clarification. Do not pretend to know what is being said. Often unfamiliar jargon and acronyms will be used. But do learn the jargon and acronyms as soon as you can.

22. Bring your child to the IEP meeting. If you feel it is inappropriate for them to stay for the entire meeting, bring your child for part of the meeting. Let them share what they need. When h/she is older, let him/her chair the meeting.

23. Consider bringing all your children to the IEP meeting so they can support their sibling.

Why did I bring Ieva's brothers to her IEP meeting beginning in the second grade? Did they understand the meeting? Well...not entirely. However, they knew I was always attending meetings and I wanted to take away some of the mystery. Also, I wanted my sons to see how I advocated for my daughter. I wanted them to witness how one individual could stand up for an idea, even if everyone in the room disagreed. I am preparing them to grow up and hopefully become co-advocates with their sister, who I am grooming to become a self-advocate. It's okay with me if they attend the IEP meeting to escape going to science. It's okay with me if they attend the IEP meeting just because I am feeding them organic coconut milk and multigrain bagels. ~Anne Treimanis

24. If you are curious as to what happens to a boy who goes to his sister's IEP meetings...this is how one story unfolds. In an effort to continue advocacy training, I brought my son to a disability related rally in Washington, DC. He knew the purpose of the rally, but admittedly I had to sell it as a day off of school with some sightseeing. He agreed to go, figuring that the rally piece was something he had to put up with. To this day he speaks positively about the rally and remembers the lessons he learned there.

25. Consider inviting other students to the IEP meeting. Kids often have great ideas on how to support students. Of course, your child needs to be okay with this:

Ieva has invited a couple of friends to her IEP meetings. At first, they were too shy to speak up. During

particular parts of the IEP meetings, I asked them if they thought a certain plan would work. When discussing certain issues, I asked the students what they thought the problem was or what their ideas were. By purposely including them in the conversation, not only did they feel valued but they surprised everyone with good insights. Remember, the students do not have to stay for the entire meeting.
~Anne Treimanis

26. Student Strengths: An educational program is effective when it is based on the student's strengths and considers his/her interests to help strengthen challenge areas. For instance, a child that is very athletic can use team sports as an avenue to build social skills.

27. Never, never, never go to an IEP alone! The person you bring does not necessarily have to be a trained advocate, h/she can be someone who cares about your child and family. If necessary, ask them not to speak. Just having them there, writing notes will let the district know that you take your rights seriously.

TIPS ON ADVOCATES

1. When you choose an advocate, make sure that h/she is prepared.

2. Ask your advocate what kind of training h/she received. Hopefully h/she has been to a Wrightslaw training. The gold standard for advocacy training is COPAA's SEAT program. Learn about COPAA at http://www.copaa.org.

3. Make sure the person presents him or herself in a professional manner.

4. Make sure that the advocate shares your views on inclusive education.

5. Some advocates bring their own anger to the table. Choose someone who is diplomatic but strong.

6. Do not forego preparation for the IEP meeting because you "trust" your advocate.

7. Prepare for the meeting WITH your advocate. H/she must represent your point of view; h/she is not there to take over. This is YOUR child and YOUR meeting.

8. When preparing with your advocate, identify what is not negotiable, and what you are willing to compromise on. Prioritize your issues.

9. Make sure your advocate has a copy of and has read all of your child's records.

10. Do not hire an advocate one day before the meeting. The advocate will not have enough time to read the records and prepare properly with you.

11. If you cannot afford an advocate, think about making an exchange agreement with another parent of a child who has an IEP. If h/she goes to your child's IEP meeting, you will attend his/her child's IEP meeting.

1. Record your IEP meeting. You will have a completely accurate record of the meeting and you will be free to listen and participate in the meeting rather than writing notes.

2. Let the school know ahead of time that you will be recording. Most schools will want to have their own recorder running too and this gives them notice that they will need to have a recorder. Do not ask them; send an email politely stating that you intend to record. You can say, "Dear Team, I am very much looking forward to our upcoming IEP meeting, which will be held on behalf of my daughter. I intend to record this meeting so that I may fully participate in the process. Thank you, Ms. Parent."

3. Get a tote bag to hold your recorder with fresh batteries. If you are using your phone or iPad to record, make sure it is fully charged.

4. Don't keep the recorder next to you. Put it in the middle of the table, but not so far that you cannot monitor it.

5. When the meeting is over, do not immediately turn the recorder off. Keep it running. Critical details are often discussed after the IEP meeting is officially over. Keep the recorder on if you leave the room for a while.

6. Listen to the recording! You'll be surprised at how much you have missed!

7. If you are going to be involved in a due process hearing, have all of your IEP meeting tapes transcribed. You can do this yourself, or hire a professional transcriber. If you transcribe the tape on your own, double space and always state who is speaking. Number the pages. If you use the tape at a hearing, submit the tape with the transcription. The tape will be your evidence; the transcription will be an aid to understanding the tape.

8. Remember that a recording is an educational record, under both IDEA and FERPA, and is subject to the confidentiality requirements of the regulations.

9. Get comfortable your recording device. If you record on your tablet or phone or on a digital recorder, make sure you know how to upload it onto your computer. Then you can store the audio file or send it to someone to transcribe.

10. Register as an employer at http://www.upwork.com. You can hire freelancers from around the world to transcribe the recordings, for just a few dollars an hour. Check out http://www.fiverr.com for low cost transcribing.

IF YOU ARE STILL USING OLD-SCHOOL TAPE RECORDERS

1. If you are using an old-style tape recorder, make sure you have extra tapes.

2. The tape packages should already be opened so you are not fumbling around trying to get the wrapper off.

3. Have the labels already marked. Otherwise, you may start taping over your own tape.

4. Mark the labels, "Ivy Smith's IEP, date, tape one of ___."

5. Start with fresh batteries and bring extras.

6. Also bring an extra tape recorder. I have seen meetings stopped because the school could not find their own tape recorder. Or, in the interest of collaboration, offer to make copies of your tapes.

7. Don't rely on a cord, there may not be an empty outlet. Also, the cord might be too short, and you don't want to create a distraction by using a big extension cord.

8. Use a regular sized cassette recorder and not the microcassette recorder; small microcassettes do not produce the same quality sound and they are not as sensitive as full size cassette tapes.

9. Don't buy low end blank tapes. These cheaper tapes will stretch more easily, especially when they are in fast-forwarded or rewound.

10. Make sure your recorder makes a noise when it shuts off. You don't want to have the meeting running if the tape has stopped, nor do you want to watch the clock to guess how much more time you have.

11. Buy the longest playing tapes to avoid switching often. You can also consider bringing someone to the meeting whose job it will be to watch the tape, and turn it to the other side when necessary. You might forget to do it.

12. When you get home, if you are using an old fashioned cassette tape, break the tabs to prevent someone from taping over the tape.

13. Fugget about it! Scrap these tape recording tips. Ditch the cassettes and go digital!

TIPS ON WHAT TO DO AFTER THE IEP MEETING

1. Always debrief with your advocate, spouse, or whoever accompanied you immediately after the meeting. Write down what you remember, and then add your own opinions. Then write a thank you note for the time people spent meeting about your child. Use the note to document key decisions and to review the issues that are still unresolved.

2. After you receive the Prior Written Notice, prepare a document called "Parent Response to the IEP." Go through the IEP line by line and correct all typos, mistakes, and inaccuracies. Also write what was omitted from the IEP document.

3. If there is serious discrepancy between what occurred at the IEP meeting and what was included in the IEP, consider adding the phrase, "Please append this to the IEP document" or "please include a copy of this letter to my child's special education file."

4. In a perfect world, you would have made dinner ahead of time so it is waiting in the crockpot. Give yourself a break that evening. Spend some quality time with your family without staring at your cell phone. Enjoy your children – no matter what they are like. Think about lighting a candle. Maybe treat yourself to a glass of wine. Or a bottle.

5. If things don't work out, consider filing a Compliance Complaint to your state department of education, if the school does not provide the services they agreed to in the IEP.

6. If you cannot agree with the IEP, you can file for a Due Process Hearing. You can file for a Due Process Hearing if you and the School District cannot agree on eligibility, placement, FAPE, program needs, least restrictive environment (LRE), or related services. At the hearing both parties present evidence to an independent hearing officer who will decide on the facts and the law and issue a written decision. You cannot file to sue a teacher or administrator personally under IDEA. You cannot sue for damages. There is no private right of action under IDEA.

1. Insure that each proposed goal is measurable, and is based on your child's evaluations.

2. Determine the criteria that will be used to evaluate whether or not goals were met. These criteria must be completely clear and understandable to all team members, including you. If the team recommends a criteria of "80% or more" ask that this be explained. Is it that the child will perform the task correctly 80% of the school day? Or is the child going to perform 80% of the task correctly every day? Or is the child going to perform the task correctly 4 out of 5 days of the week? Or will the child perform the task 80% of the time in any given hour that data is collected? This needs to be crystal clear to every team member since this is the measure that will be used to determine if the child has successfully acquired a skill.

3. Think about prompting levels. Skills may not be practical if prompts are always required.

4. Think about the child being able to use the skill "across all settings." A skill may not be practical if the child only masters it in the resource room.

5. If behavior impedes learning, make sure that a positive behavior plan is put in place. A positive behavior plan is based on a "functional behavior analysis," which is a way of looking at

the causes of behavior as well as the aspects of a child's learning environment that may be contributing to the behavior.

6. The IEP must clearly and specifically state where services are to take place. Do not agree to "in the classroom OR in the resource room, as appropriate." This will leave the decision of where to provide services up to the therapist or implementer, and leaves the door open for the service to be provided where it is more convenient for staff, rather than what is best for the child.

7. Consider asking for support for the teacher and other staff members that work with your child. The law allows you to request services that are provided to the parents or teachers of a child with a disability to help them to more effectively work with your child. This might include training about your child's disability for the teacher so h/she can work more effectively to include and educate your child.

8. Consider asking for support for you as a parent to work with your child.

9. The law allows for parent counseling and training to assist parents in understanding the special needs of their child, provide parents with information about child development and help parents to acquire the necessary skills that will allow them to support the implementation of their child's IEP or IFSP.

10. Remember that test results are not always valid or reliable. They are merely a snapshot of a certain moment of time in your

child's life. Some tests are not appropriate for a child based on his/her disability. Make sure to ask questions about this.

11. When deciding on placement, the first choice for every single child must be the general education curriculum in the school and classroom h/she would attend if they had been born without a disability. Make sure that the correct sequence of steps is followed in deciding on placement. Placement decisions should NEVER:

- Be made based on a child's label ("Paul has cerebral palsy so he'll go to Room 5 where all the kids with CP go")
- Be made before the IEP is developed
- Be based on administrative convenience (because all the special education teachers and related personnel are located in one school)

12. Placement decisions should ALWAYS:

- Be made by the IEP team, not one or two members of the team
- Be reviewed at least annually
- Parents should be allowed to view placement

13. Consider how related services can be integrated within the school day and not become a pull-out service:

> Related services, such as transportation and such developmental, corrective, and other supportive services as are required to assist a child with a disability to benefit from special education. The

evaluation process will help the team determine what related services the student needs. Think about how those related services can be provided in the general education environment. For example, if the speech teacher wants to facilitate pragmatic language skills, couldn't that be done over lunchtime in the cafeteria? No, I don't mean a "lunch bunch" with six students, all receiving special education services. I mean a typical lunch group with the speech therapist seated nearby. Articulation goals can be met during a foreign language class, when everyone is struggling with new words. And what about physical therapy? Should students be practicing going up and down stairs that lead to nowhere, in order to perfect the alternating feet movements? Could the PT meet the student in the hallways when the students really are going upstairs? The PT could also meet the student at recess or during gym and work on skills and avoid the "pull-out" model. Don't think that related services is something that a therapist has to do to a student in a private room and then hope that the skills transfers over. It's not just an effort to "fix" a child by doing related services three times a week for 20 minutes. Related services can be taught in natural environments, empowering students to do real things in real settings. Look across all of the school settings. Think of how related services personnel can help students in places that they already are in. ~Anne Treimanis

14. Plan for recreational activities to promote social inclusion and to help the student make friends.

15. Consider assistive technology. The law requires that a discussion of assistive technology needs be conducted for every child as part of their IEP.

16. Classes that have a disproportionate number of students with disabilities, sometimes called "transitional classes" or reverse mainstream classes, are not inclusive classes. These are special education placements. If you want your child in a regular class placement, do not agree to a class with a disproportionate number of children with disabilities. Inclusive classes follow the law of natural proportions, whereby the school and classroom reflect the community at large. If 10% of the people in your community have disabilities, then the classroom should contain no more then 10% of the students with disabilities.

17. If your child will be transitioning out of public schools, consider post-secondary school options. Even kids with significant cognitive disabilities are attending colleges. College courses can be modified, accommodations can be offered. Section 504 of the Rehabilitation Act of 1974 and the Americans with Disabilities Act (ADA) will offer legal protections and ethical guidance. If your child attends the graduation ceremony with his or her classmates but does not get a diploma, the public school district can support your child in a post-secondary option.

18. Insure that the role of the paraprofessional for your child is clear. Make sure that a good plan is in place so the paraprofessional does not become your child's "private

teacher," teaching your child while the classroom teacher instructs the rest of the class. Clarify the roles of each adult in the classroom. Make sure the teacher has established a method to communicate his/her daily expectations and lesson plans for the entire class.

19. It's not okay to watch your child walking down the hallway without a backpack, with the paraprofessional following him/her with a backpack, project, and waters. The paraprofessional is not your child's valet, promoting learned helplessness.

20. If a student uses augmentative or alternative communication (AAC), make sure the communication system is always readily available. If someone needs to assist the student, make sure other students, not only the teacher, can assist. Make sure the entire school gets the opportunity to be involved with the AAC. When a teacher communicates with the student, it should be in a respectful manner so the teacher can serve as a role model to other students.

21. Remember, the 'I' in IEP stands for INDIVIDUAL. Write an IEP that is individually tailored to your child's strengths and needs. Do not allow the school to pick from a menu and give you a McIEP. The IEP must be individualized, specially designed, to meet the unique educational needs of each student.

22. Ask your child what they want in their IEP. Believe in your child. Encourage them to make choices and take control. Listen to the voice of a student.

1. Please know that a related service is a service provided by the school district that enables your child to benefit from special education. The most common related services for children on IEP's are Occupational Therapy (OT), Physical Therapy (PT), and Speech Therapy (SLP).

2. Do not forget that Transportation is a related service. It's not okay for the school to ignore bus problems because "that's an issue for the transportation company."

3. The school district is required to identify who will be providing the related service, as well as the amount of time and frequency of the service. Be mindful that the IEP can read that the OT will be responsible for OT services, but the OTA (OT Assistant) will be implementing them. Also, your child might receive SLP services, but they might be in a group of 5. Be sure to ask questions about the size of the group and who will be implementing the service.

4. If the school district wants to talk about or decrease related services, consider the following:
- Inform the IEP team verbally and in writing that you disagree with their decision.
- Request a prior written notice from the school district regarding what data was used to arrive at their decision.

- Consider paying for a private evaluation by a therapist that is not affiliated with the school district. You may invite the private evaluator to attend, in person or by phone conference, your child's IEP meeting to discuss their findings. The school district is required to consider all findings of the outside evaluator.
- Consider exercising your procedural safeguard rights.

5. It's not appropriate to determine what related services will be granted on the basis of available therapists or a therapist's schedule or caseload! Insist that your child's related services be determined using data.

6. If the school district does not have a provider for the related service, then request that they contract with an outside agency.

TRACKING IEP PROGRESS

1. Make sure the IEP contains built-in methods to communicate with school staff. For example, ask for scheduled planning time each week so the general education teachers can plan modifications with the Special Education teachers. You should ask to be allowed to attend those meetings once every four to eight weeks. You can also ask for monthly team-meetings to discuss issues and have a communication journal go back and forth each day:

> *Understand that the modification planning time should not be used to discuss other issues that should be reserved for the monthly team meeting or a separate*

conference. If curriculum planning does not occur then that week may not be successful.
~Anne Treimanis

2. Volunteer at the school. Get to know the players. Watch what is going on and develop information sources.

3. Find or cultivate an "inside advocate:"

> *Ideally, one of the members of the IEP team should serve as your "inside" or "school based" advocate. It's the one professional who consistently disregards hidden school agendas or the inflexible nature of a school bureaucracy and thinks about what is best for your child. My "inside" advocate will remain silent when the school gives me the "party line;" then, after the meeting I will find out what really happened or who was being the gatekeeper. My inside advocates have not been disloyal staff, they are professionals who are deeply invested in my child's success and do not fear collaborating with me. Some inside advocates will never openly align themselves with the parent, but they are always watching out for the student.*
> *~Anne Treimanis*

4. Seek out information about your child from other parents who may visit the school as well peers at school. Many children with disabilities—particularly young children—will not be able to give you an accurate report of their day. You may need to be creative to gather information about what is happening with your child at school.

5. If possible, avoid the bus and pick up your child every day.

> This tip can really inconvenience your life! I know, I picked up my children for several years, each and every day. Why did I do it? In addition to avoiding bus issues, I was able to have daily contact with the teacher or teaching assistant. Every day I arrived at school 5 minutes before dismissal. My body was always in the same spot. When my kids appeared, I read their faces so I know what kind of day it had been.
> ~Anne Treimanis

6. Don't ever trust the school 100%, no matter how nice and caring they are. When things are going well and even if your child is successfully included, it's not time to nap. Stay forever vigilant. They are not your friends; this is a business relationship.

7. Be sure that IEP goals are measurable.

TIPS ON WRITING MEASURABLE GOALS

1. You should be able to easily understand how a child's progress is being measured. For example, "Louisa will improve in reading" is not measurable. An example of a measurable annual goal would be, "Given 48 minutes of small group instruction using the Wilson Program with closely matched peers on a daily basis, Louisa will progress from a 4.2 grade reading level to a 5.6 reading level as measured by the WADE Assessment (Wilson *Assessment* for Decoding and Encoding)."

2. When percentages are used to report progress, be sure there is enough information to clearly explain what is being measured and how. For example, if you are told that your child forms their letters with 80% accuracy, does that mean that 80% of the time all the letters are formed accurately, or 8 out of 10 letters are formed accurately, or something else entirely?

3. Be sure that measures are objective. It is not helpful to hear that your child is "improving" if you have nothing concrete to refer to. If work samples will be used to assess progress, sit down with the teacher to review exactly how the work is evaluated. For example, are errors counted? Is there a rubric? Is there a point system? and so on.

4. Ask your child's teachers and related service personnel to paraphrase and summarize reports rather than reading them word for word at the IEP meeting. If there is anything in the report that you do not understand, say so. Reports should contain an absolute minimum of jargon. If clinical terms are unavoidable, ask the evaluator to include a written explanation of the unfamiliar term in layman's language.

5. Insist that reports and evaluations include recommendations. It is not acceptable that the report ends with "recommendations will be discussed at the IEP meeting." Educators have confessed to me that they are instructed not to write recommendations because then the school district will be responsible for implementing/paying for them.

6. Don't set the bar too low when writing goals. It is common for goals and objectives to target a 70% or 80% success rate but think carefully about how the goal plays out in real life. If a goal states that a child will speak in a respectful tone of voice to adults with 70% accuracy that means that 30% of the time (almost 2 hours out of the school day!) the child is disrespectful.

7. Don't wait for the annual review to assess whether the child is making acceptable progress. With a measurable goal, you will know whether or not the instructional plan is working early enough to make adjustments. For example, if the annual goal states that Chelsea will progress one year in her math skills, and at the first quarter she has made only one month of progress (as measured by an objective assessment tool) then it is clear that the instructional plan does not meet Chelsea's needs and must be amended or fortified. When a child isn't progressing as expected, the approach should be "what can we do differently" NOT the assumption that the child can't achieve the goal. Don't allow the school to revise the goal downward; instead up the services so they can master the goal.

8. Overall, look for these attributes in a goal:
    *   Who? The student for whom the goal is written.
    *   Will do what? The observable behavior describing what the student will do to complete the goal.
    *   To what level or degree? Criteria states how many times the behavior must be observed for the goal to be considered completed. Mastery states the level of achievement required for mastery.

- Under what conditions? Conditions include a description of the situation, setting, or given material that will need to be in place for the goal to be completed.
- In what length of time? The timeframe to complete the goal.
- How will progress be measured? This is the performance data.

POSTSECONDARY TRANSITION IEPS

1. Parents, NEVER blink your eyes. If you do, your young children will be aging out of public school and moving forward into the rest of their lives.

2. Never forget that the purpose of special education is to "To ensure that all children with disabilities have available to them a free appropriate public education that emphasizes special education and related services designed to meet their unique needs and prepare them for further education, employment, and independent living." (Sec. 300.1 Purposes). Therefore, when the school wants to graduate your child and exit them out of special education services, you should ask the following three questions: Is h/she ready to go to college? Is h/she ready to work? Is h/she ready to live on his own? If the answer is no, then services should continue until the student ages out.

3. When you think about the purposes of special education, you will know if the supports and services you are requesting are appropriate.

4. It is important to learn "life skills." But every time your child is pulled into a life skills class to learn how to shop or do laundry, it is at the expense of something else in the general education curriculum. Sometimes it's good to be practical. For example, when a child graduates from school, their parents can pay someone minimum wage to teach him/her how to clean and shop; or the parents can do it. Or the parents can pay a highly qualified reading tutor $100 an hour to teach their child how to read. So does it make sense to cut back on the reading program in school to learn how to shop at Walmart? I think not.

5. Consider having your high school child sign up for the cooking class, to learn how to cook from a real cooking teacher, instead of covering cooking in the life skills class. Do not feel intimidated simply because your child may need significant modifications to be successful in this class (or any class).

6. Get familiar with some of the countless number of formal assessments available for determining transition needs.

7. If the school's "one size fits all" transition program for all students with the label of Intellectual Disability (ID) or Autism Spectrum Disorder (ASD) is the only program offered, remind yourself that the I in IEP stands for individualized.

8. If you and your child make a decision to defer a legal graduation, please know that s/he will still take their senior photos, go to the prom, and participate in the graduation ceremony.

9. Consider deferring "life skills" until the student completes Grade 12 and then moves on to a transition program. Consider that becoming a "super senior" or returning to the high school building is embarrassing and inappropriate. Check out http://www.thinkcollege.net to see what programs might be suitable for your child.

10. When evaluating whether or not a transition program will be appropriate for your child, consider ALL of your child's needs that conform with the purposes of IDEA. Use my Transition Skills check list in Appendix 10. If you see skills that your child does not have, include those in a Parent Concern list that you will present prior to the IEP meeting.

"Separate educational facilities are inherently unequal"
~ Supreme Court - Brown v. Board of Education

ENSURING ACCESS TO THE GENERAL CURRICULUM

To the maximum extent appropriate, children with disabilities...are educated with children who are not disabled, and special classes, separate schooling, or other removal of children with disabilities from the regular educational environment occurs only when the nature or severity of the disability of a child is such that education in regular classes with the use of supplementary aids and services cannot be achieved satisfactorily.
~ The Individuals with Disabilities Act § 300.114 LRE requirements.

1. Start out by asking if the student can do the lesson the same way as the rest of the class. Don't assume that every lesson will need to be modified.

2. Only use one-to-one adult assistance if you have already tried less restrictive supports, such as small group learning, peer tutoring, augmentative communication, picture schedules, and so on.

3. Build collaboration time between special education and regular education personnel into the IEP to be sure there is time to adequately plan modifications.

4. Use picture schedules for young children to avoid dependence on adults to tell them what is coming next. This allows the student to predict their day and allays anxiety.

5. To begin to teach independent organizational skills, color code loose papers in middle schoolers' planners by subject. For example, all science papers have a red dot on the top, social studies papers have a green dot, and so on so that the student can independently file and organize their planner.

6. Teach problem solving skills to children so that they can participate in modifying lessons for diverse groups. For example, have small groups of students brainstorm as many ways as possible to teach a lesson.

7. Keep good records of modified lessons so they are available for other students who may have similar learning needs.

8. When modifying students work, be sure to maintain the core idea of the lesson. For example, if you are reading a story, assigning only some of the pages would prevent the student from answering comprehension questions related to the entire story. Try books on tape or scanned text so the student learns the most important content.

9. Follow a continuum when modifying work.
   - Some examples: Can the student do what the rest of the class is doing? If not, then:

- Can the student be given extra cues or prompts (such as highlighted text, or verbal prompts from teacher) to accomplish the goals of the lesson? If not, then:
- Can the student get assistance from a peer to complete the lesson? If not, then:
- Can the student work in a cooperative learning group with adult assistance? If not, then:
- Can the student work on the same lesson with direct adult assistance? If not then:
- Can the student work on a modified version of the lesson, accomplishing the most important objectives of the lesson? If not, then:
- Can the student work on an alternate activity that accomplishes the goals of the lesson? And so on.

10. Use the principles of universal design to create plans that will meet the needs of a diverse group of students. Universal design is the design of activities and environments to be usable by all students, to the greatest extent possible, without the need for adaptation or modification. For example, for all literature lessons, have stories available in print, on tape, in scanned computerized text, in large print text, Braille, with additional pictures to accompany the text, a video or movie of the story, a script to act out the story, and with text available at a variety of grade levels. This way you won't have to "redo the wheel" every time a student enters your class with specialized learning needs.

11. Pay attention to the environment. Some children may need to move around more than other children, or may need quiet space to work without distractions. Also consider special seating, study carrels, providing space for movement or breaks, standing desks, or providing help to organize work space.

12. Consider testing accommodations to be sure students have a chance to demonstrate what they know. For example allowing answers to be dictated, allowing additional time, reading test to student, accepting short answers, or highlighting key directions.

13. Consider behavioral supports such as providing rest breaks, teaching the child how to make friends, administering a functional behavioral analysis, and teaching independence skills.

14. Consider the theory of multiple intelligences from Howard Gartner when planning lessons for diverse learners.

15. Some activities under the eight "intelligences" include:
- Linguistic- read about it, write about it, talk about it, and listen to it.
- Logical-Mathematical- quantify it, think critically about it, conceptualize it.
- Visual-Spatial- see it, draw it, visualize it, color it, mind-map it.
- Bodily-Kinesthetic- build it, act it out, touch it, get a gut feeling of it, dance it.
- Musical- sing it, rap it, listen to it.

- Interpersonal- teach it, collaborate on it, interact with respect to it.
- Intrapersonal- connect it to your personal life, make choices with regard to it.
- Naturalist- sense it, feel it, experience it, relate it, think globally about it, be an activist about it.

16. Don't feel like you are taking a disproportionate share of resources when insisting on a quality education for your child. Remember that there are reciprocal benefits of inclusive education. All children benefit from inclusive education.

MORE TIPS TO ENSURE ACCESS

1. Read the TASH resolution on Inclusive Education. Read it again when you are feeling isolated or tired. Check http://www.tash.org. Or, choose to write your own resolutions. Read material not only to empower yourself with skills and ammunition, but to edify and motivate you.

2. Begin a dialogue with the administration to support staff training and ongoing professional development opportunities in Inclusive Education and curriculum modification.

3. Administrators can support teachers by providing in-service training, and allow teachers to attend conferences and seminars. Administrators can make sure teachers have time to collaborate with each other and have time to modify and adapt the curriculum. Send thank you notes to administrators who

support inclusive education. Work with administrators, bringing in-service opportunities to their attention. Ask for this at the IEP meeting.

4. If a paraprofessional is spending some or all of the day with your child, make sure you have built in communication opportunities with him/her.

5. Ask the paraprofessional to write into your child's home/school journal every day. Make sure h/she is invited to team meetings. Insure that training opportunities are made available to him/her.

6. If a paraprofessional is spending some or all of the day with your child, make sure h/she receives ongoing professional development opportunities. Invite him/her to conferences and seminars. Give him/her books and literature to read. Make sure the paraprofessional is invited to all of the team meetings and IEP meetings. Have your IEP include training for the paraprofessionals.

7. When planning Extended School Year, do not settle for the "One Size Fits All" program. Consider typical activities with supports and services.

8. Be sure that classrooms have a quiet space for children who need a break from noise and activity. Some ideas for limiting noise include:
- Have a set time for students to use the electric pencil sharpener.

- Use digital timers instead of loud kitchen timers.
- Allow physically active students to kneel or stand by their desks.
- Place easily distracted students near hardworking children in the center of the room.
- Have a quiet corner where students can work and read on beanbags on the floor.

9. If a student needs help with organization, consider the following:

- Allow student to have a second set of books for home.
- Some teachers assign a buddy to check if the student turned in homework and reports, and then wrote down the next day's assignments in the student planner. I am not sure if I like the power differential. Instead, can the homework be emailed to the parent and then have the parent check on the planner?
- Make sure the student has a friend to call if he forgets what homework to do.
- Make sure you own a fax machine so friends can fax assignments. If you don't want to have an extra phone line or fax machine, subscribe to faxes that come directly onto your computer. I use Ring Central for this service.
- Ask the school to upload HW sheets electronically so they are accessible on the computer.
- Ask that a teacher or teaching assistant meet the student before or after school, or some other time, to

privately meet with student and help organize his locker one day, and his backpack another day.

1. Transportation is a related service, if a student needs it to access education. It must be looked at carefully. The following are some bus tips.

2. Give the child an assigned seat near the driver (although the driver keeps his eyes on the road and realistically can't do much supervising).

3. Install a camcorder in every bus to see what really goes on. In districts that have done this, incidents have dropped dramatically. Camcorders are really inexpensive these days. It's okay when they break, the kids won't know it.

4. Ask the principal to board the bus just before it takes off to "settle" the kids.

5. Assign the older students to be bus patrol. It's a privilege for the higher grades. The kids get to wear an orange band across their chests and they rotate turns, one month at a time. If they abuse their responsibilities, they lose the privilege of monitoring.

6. Assign a rotating buddy for the student that needs some support.

7. Allow the student to wear headphones and listen to music if it helps him/her stay out of trouble or remain calm.

8. Find out, through an auditory evaluation and a sensory integration evaluation, if the bus environment is troubling to the student.

9. Change the bus route so a student can have a shorter ride.

10. Make sure the bus rules are clear and understood by all who ride.

11. Ask the bus driver to post the rules in the bus, using pictures as well as words.

12. Create social stories (using Carol Gray's book as a guide) to help deal with bus scenarios.

13. Consider picking up your child every day from school. You will have important daily contact with the teachers.

> Let's face it; a bus ride is merely 50 unsupervised kids for 10 to 45 minutes. That's a recipe for trouble, even with careful planning. There are no skills to be learned; in the real world we do not ride a bus with 50 kids. Additionally, the bus is where the worst teasing takes place. The truth is, a bus ride is a situation no sane mother ever would voluntarily orchestrate. There is no educational value in a bus ride. The only time an adult will repeat their school bus riding experience is if they become a schoolteacher and take field trips. Typical city buses are not loaded with students, so the skills will not transfer to real life. One time, for my

own daughter, we agreed to the little segregated school bus. We negotiated a deal in which not only my daughter was picked up, but my sons and all the other children in our cul-de-sac as well. They loved the private service.
~Anne Treimanis

TIPS ON HOW TO GROW INCLUSION MINDED STAFF

1. Provide books to the teachers on inclusion and other disability related matters. Give books as end of year or holiday gifts instead of gift certificates for a manicure.

2. Make sure each staff member personally hears about training opportunities.

3. If you get a flyer on a seminar or conference, make sure the information is personally put into each team member's hand. Don't just give the school one copy of an upcoming seminar and hope they circulate it. Make several copies and insure that each individual connected with your child gets a copy. Ask him/her directly if they would be interested in attending. Post flyers on a bulletin board. Email it to the staff.

4. In your child's IEP document, under teacher supports, negotiate that your child's teachers will attend at least two training opportunities on inclusive education.

5. Make sure the community learns about training opportunities and disability related events. Write press releases about upcoming events and fax or email it to all of the local

papers. Buy a fax machine, or better yet, subscribe to RingCentral (sending faxes through your computer). Create a list of fax numbers of newspapers, advocacy groups, and disability related organizations. Put that list in a protective plastic sleeve, and keep it next to the fax machine at all times. Or store your lists electronically. Collect emails for organizations and community leaders. Always pass on information. Everyone needs to be kept in the loop; we need to stand on each other's shoulders to create inclusive communities.

6. Create a bulletin board in each school where information about disability related events could be posted for parents and staff to view. Keep it updated. If there are several schools in your district, find someone in each school that can update the bulletin board.

7. Find out how each individual on the team likes to communicate. Some teachers prefer e-mail, others like to speak on the phone in the evening, and some prefer a note. If your child cannot reliably deliver notes via their backpack, consider faxing it. All teachers have mailboxes at school. If you fax a letter, someone in the office will put it in the teacher's mailbox. This method might compromise some privacy, as office staff or parent volunteers could read the letter before it reaches the teacher's mailbox. I prefer email because emails live on the school's server and are not destroyed.

8. Learn to use technology to make your advocacy work easier. Start developing lists of contacts that you can quickly and efficiently get information out to. Create a website or Facebook page just for disability related seminars in your county. As a parent, you can bring new and innovative programs and changes that will impact students and promote inclusion. You are there for the long haul and are deeply invested in the quality of education in your district. You have the time, commitment and energy to overhaul the system. If you remain committed to a vision of fully inclusive schools, you can effectuate change and the administration will be riding on your coattails.

> *I created a website for my little part of the world. It has grown to become known as "one-stop shopping" for people who want to know where to go for local training, how to contact our local resources, and where to find general as well as very local information. Check http://www.spednet.org to see what was done.*
> *~Anne Treimanis*

> *Remember, the purpose of an evaluation is to either determine that a student is eligible for special education services* **or** *to provide relevant information to the general education teacher on how to effectively teach the student in the general education environment. It is not simply to generate numbers or scores.*
> *~Anne Treimanis*

TIPS ON PLANNING AN EVALUATION

1. Be sure you are comfortable with all tests or evaluations recommended for your child. The law requires that you sign a release for all evaluations. Speak to your pediatrician, a representative of a parent group, or an advocacy organization about tests recommended for your child so you are both knowledgeable and comfortable with the evaluation process.

2. Remember that a "screening" is NOT an evaluation. It's simply a superficial screening to see if an evaluation is warranted.

3. In some instances, you may opt to arrange for a private evaluator rather than consent to the school district evaluator administering a particular test or assessment. Some reasons parents may choose this option include;

- When you want to control what information is included in your child's permanent school file: Some psychological testing may include a detailed family history and you may wish to keep information not directly related to your child's education out of their school record.

- When you are not confident that the proposed test will be an accurate measure of your child's ability: Some intelligence testing does not capture the true abilities of children who are non-verbal or who have difficulty communicating. You may wish to choose an evaluator who is skilled in administering non-verbal IQ tests.

- When you are not confident in the training or skill of the evaluator: Many parents mistakenly assume that all school psychologists are Ph.D. level practitioners or that all Occupational Therapists have been trained in sensory integration techniques. This is not necessarily true. You may wish to choose an evaluator whose skill or training exceeds the minimum qualifications of school district personnel.

- Remember, schools do not diagnose students. They only make them eligible for special education. If you want to truly understand your child's issues, you will need private testing that provides diagnostic impressions. When securing such testing, ask in advance, if the person who is testing has the clinical credentials to diagnose a child. If not, look elsewhere.

4. Remember that if you choose to bypass the school evaluator in favor of a private evaluator, you will be responsible for paying for the evaluation. It is important to share relevant data with the IEP team for use in planning your child's program.

TIPS FOR PARENTS ON GETTING GOOD READING PROGRAMS AND HELPING THEIR CHILDREN BECOME GOOD READERS

1. Understand that Students who get the best educational programs tend to be those who have the most empowered parents.

2. How can parents help their child develop reading skills?
   - Show your child through your actions that you value reading.
   - Have a variety of reading materials in your home.
   - Bring along a book or magazine everywhere you go, including vacations, car trips, and medical appointments.
   - Read to your child regularly.
   - Encourage meaningful writing activities. Have your child write a shopping list, a thank you letter, or a to-do list.
   - Set the bar high.
   - Encourage vocabulary development by using new words while engaging in interesting conversations.

3. Go to seminars, go online, and take classes on reading.

4. You MUST become an expert in reading. If your child had leukemia you would become a cancer expert. If your child is not a proficient reader, you MUST understand reading.

5. Understand the laws that protect your child.

6. Your participation on the IEP team is critical. However, it must be meaningful. Get copies of reading evaluations and proposed reading goals prior to the IEP meeting.

7. Make sure that the reading goals are measurable. Instead of "Zak will improve his reading, demonstrating one year's growth," consider "By May 15th, Zak will be able to read a passage of text orally at the 8.2 grade equivalent level as measured by the GORT- 5 (Gray Oral Reading Test)."

8. If your child has the label of ID and is having difficulty decoding, do not accept a sight word program like Edmark or Reading Milestones. Such interventions do not teach critical phonetic concepts, necessary to "sound out" – and spell – unmemorized words. Most likely your child will require a program that uses the Orton-Gillingham methodology.

9. Work with local parent groups to arrange for seminars and conferences on reading in your area.

10. Request a reading evaluation for your child. The reading subtests of the Woodcock Johnson IV (WCJ IV) or the Wechsler Individual Achievement Test (WIAT) do not, in themselves, constitute a reading evaluation – and frequently the information they provide are of little value for a student with an intellectual disability. Use the template in Appendix 11 when asking for a reading evaluation (thanks in large part to Wrightslaw.com for this letter).

11. Ask the following four questions about your child's reading program:

- Does my child's reading program contain the five components of instruction recommended by the National Reading Panel?
- Is the bar set high enough?
- Is the person implementing the reading intervention qualified? What training has s/he received?
- Is the child getting systematic, explicit instruction in reading?

12. The National Reading Panel identified five critical areas that effective reading instruction must address (Phonemic Awareness, Phonics, Fluency, Vocabulary, and Text Comprehension). You MUST understand the five components of reading! They are described more fully in Appendix 12.

TIPS FOR ATTORNEYS AND ADVOCATES ON GETTING GOOD READING PROGRAMS

1. LEARN THE TOOLS OF THE TRADE!!! Go to seminars, go online, and take classes on reading. Understanding reading will help you spot issues when advocating for your clients.

2. Two great publications are: Put Reading First: Kindergarten through Grade 3, and Put Reading First: Helping Your Child Learn To Read: A Parent Guide: Preschool Through Grade Three. Get these free publications at https://www.edpubs.gov.

I attended a 16 hour COPPA Pre-Conference course in Orton-Gillingham methodology and it forever changed the way I practiced law. Let's face it, if you were a medical malpractice attorney, you would need to understand a few things about the human body! Similarly, if you engage in special education law, you MUST understand the fundamentals of reading. Otherwise you'll be bamboozled by the school district just like the parents are.
~Anne Treimanis

3. Understand the qualifications and recommendations of the National Reading Panel. Learn more at https://www.nichd.nih.gov/research/supported/Pages/nrp.aspx

4. If your client is not a proficient reader, do NOT assume it's due to his/her disability. Ask the parents to request a comprehensive reading evaluation, performed by a qualified reading specialist (see template at Appendix 11).

5. If your child or client has Down syndrome and is not a proficient reader, RUN to the website https://openbooksopendoors.com for the best resources.

6. Forge strong relationships with reading specialists in your state. The input of friends and colleagues who are reading experts can be invaluable to preparing for IEP meetings.

7. Grow the local reading specialists. Most of them live in the "LD world." Help them understand that students with intellectual disabilities can become proficient decoders.

8. When a reading evaluation is completed, check the recommendations carefully. The evaluation may be accurate,

but the school reading specialist may not envision students with intellectual disabilities as readers, hence recommending a sight word program. Do not hesitate to ask for an Independent Educational Evaluation for reading.

9. Request an assistive technology (AT) evaluation to see if there are high, mid, or low level AT options that complement the client's reading program and increases access to content.

10. Remember that decoding is very distinct from comprehension. Comprehension is more closely tied to intellectual challenges; decoding ability is usually relatively independent of IQ measures.

11. Do NOT assume that special education teachers are qualified to do reading evaluations or teach reading. In many states, a highly qualified Masters level special education teacher does NOT have to take any reading classes!

12. Ask for the resume of anyone doing a reading evaluation on your student. Do not assume the "Literacy Coach" or special education teacher has credentials. If a teacher claims to be "trained" in Wilson, find out if s/he went to the 5 hour class – which essentially shows you how to use the materials – or completed the requirements to achieve certification. Similarly, a teacher cannot claim to be "Orton-Gillingham trained" unless s/he has achieved certification at the Certified level – a multi-year commitment.

13. Embedded within the specific requirements provided by IDEA guaranteeing a Free and Appropriate Public Education for students with disabilities in the Least Restrictive Environment is the provision that students, including those with significant disabilities such as ID or ASD, be given evidence-based reading programs. LRE does not require that reading be taught in the general education settings. Frequently, individual instruction or small group instruction with like peers is required in a separate setting. One of the best ways to become fully included in life is to know how to read!

14. In later grades, it is NOT appropriate for older students to give up on reading and turn to "functional" skills, such as shopping and learning to do laundry. Reading is the quintessential functional skill – necessary to obtain and retain a job, navigate transportation options, read recipes or the back of food containers, stay safe, read prescription bottles, go on Facebook, text friends, and have a chance to survive in our print-based community. As proclaimed in Connecticut's Blueprint for Reading Achievement (2000), *"Teaching children to read is a central—arguably the central—mission of formal schooling."*

TIPS ON HOW TO HANDLE DIFFICULT CONVERSATIONS

1. Learn the skill of handling difficult conversations.
   - Begin by finding things that you all agree with. Example: I know that you have found it hard to teach John because his behavior is challenging at school. I deal with these challenges every day when he comes home and it can be exhausting.
   - Use "I" statements in place of "you" statements. "I" statements state how you feel; "you" statements are critical or judgmental. Example: Say, "I am feeling that I am not a member of the team because I don't get enough information about what is going on in school" instead of "You never let me know what's going on. Why can't you ever write in our communication journal?"
   - Avoid negatives because people will feel hostile. Example: Say, "Can we try..." or "Is it possible..." Don't say, "Why won't you..."
   - Avoid dictating to the school. For example, say "Could we consider...?" Don't say, "Stop doing..."
   - Try to see things from the school's point of view, but don't compromise your principles. In some conflicts,

both sides can be right. Ask lots of questions so you can see the advantages of both points of view.

- Find some positive comments to share with the team.
- If you ask a yes or no question, the school might say NO. Instead, start a question with these words — "What would it take in order to..." In this way, the school will start brainstorming solutions instead of refusing to do something.
- Try not to yell. In fact, try lowering your voice when you are angry.

2. Distinguish between personal conflicts with staff members and disagreements about your child's education. Sometimes members of the team will disagree, but they are usually focused on what is appropriate for the child. On fewer occasions, the school staff is simply rude, tired, or simply does not like you or your child. It's usually best to try to stay diplomatic and focus on the issues. After all, as attorney Pete Wright says, "Unless you are willing to pay for a private school, your relationship with the school is like marriage with no possibility for divorce."

3. Put everything in writing. Document all conversations by either keeping contemporaneous records or following up with a letter. Here are two samples of letters you can send to document a conversation.

****

Dear Mrs. SPED teacher,

Thank you very much for meeting with me this morning. You stated that the principal advised you that my son's extended school year might be cut from 6 to 3 weeks based on recent budget concerns. I shared that the IEP team agreed that my son needed a six-week program in order not to further regress in his reading skills. You stated that you would get back to me in the next couple of weeks.

If I have misunderstood our conversation in any way, let me know by end of business day today.

Thanks,

Savvy Parent

****

Dear Teacher,

Thanks for telephoning me today. You were concerned that my son was having a tough time worrying about me since my recent illness. We agreed that we would relax the rule about no cell phones at school and allow Frank to carry one. Let me know if this is what we agreed to.

Thanks so much,

Savvy Parent

****

4. Pick your battles. Don't focus on a small mistake or misjudgment. Don't worry about small procedural violations that cause no harm. You can document them, but don't make them an issue.

5. When you are in the teacher's classroom or in an administrator's office, look for any posters or knick-knacks that have a motto or quote on it. Make a note of this motto. When dealing with the person, in an appropriate moment remind them of the motto or quote they chose to display. For example,

if the teacher is pushing for another pullout, remind her about the poster that says, "All Kids Belong."

6.   Do not be afraid of using your due process rights. But analyze the cost-benefit of doing so. Costs include but are not limited to: money to hire an attorney, money lost on missed days from work or cost of child care, cost of expert witnesses, copying costs, and emotional costs.

7.   Decide ahead of time what is non-negotiable and practice appropriate phrases to state your position. Repeat these phrases over and over each time someone argues or tries to push you to change your mind. If it is critical to your family that your child is in a regular class for all their academic subjects, you might say, "We feel that Steven can be successful in a regular education classroom with appropriate supplementary aids and services." Practice saying this ahead of time and repeat as often as necessary to make it clear that you are not flexible on this point.

8.   Practice responses to prepare for what you expect the school based team to say. Be aware of time-honored traditional lines that schools use to control the IEP process and rehearse your responses. Following are some examples, see Appendix 7 for more examples:

****

Parent: I hope you don't mind, I brought my recorder because I am not a good note-taker...

Psychologist: I thought we had a trusting relationship! Don't you trust our staff, Mrs. Smith?!

Parent: I do place a lot of trust in the school. I want to record the meeting so I make sure I hear everything, so I don't misunderstand anything and I have an accurate record to help me.

****

Principal: Remember, IDEA is not fully funded. We simply don't have the money to provide the service you are requesting for your daughter.

Parent: Our responsibility as a team is to fully comply with the law.

****

Principal: I'm sorry, we have a policy against this.

Parent: What policy is that? Please give me a copy of that policy.

****

Teacher: The law says that………….

Parent: Here is a copy of the law. Please show me where in the law it says………….

****

SPED teacher: The teacher is not trained in special education.

Parent: Inclusion is just good teaching. All teachers should use differentiated instruction to benefit all students. Let's include teacher training in Orville's IEP, since this is a service permitted through IDEA.

Principal: I cannot expect my teachers to figure out the best way to teach your daughter in every single situation.

Parent: I'm not expecting her to. This is a team effort. That's why there needs to be adequate paid planning time built into the teacher's schedule.

****

SPED Teacher: The team feels that…..

Parent: But I don't feel that way. I am a full member of the IEP team.

****

Teacher: You are too personally and emotionally involved to make a reasonable decision.

Parent: Yes, I am very personally involved. That's precisely the reason I have a lot to contribute.

****

Teacher: Your child is not ready to be in the regular classroom all day.

Parent: The law is very clear that my daughter has a right to be in the general education class and it is our responsibility to design the supports and services she needs to be successful. The law is clear that children don't have to earn the right to be in general education.

****

Principal: Our budget doesn't allow us to buy…………..for every student.

Parent: But we're not talking about every student, we are only talking about Sally and her individual needs.

****

Teacher: We love your daughter and we want what's best for her.

Parent: I don't need you to love her. I need you to teach her.

****

SPED teacher: How do you expect your child to learn Math in the general education classroom?

Parent: If you don't know, let's get a consultant to help us figure this out.

TIPS FOR FORMING EFFECTIVE PARTNERSHIPS BETWEEN FAMILIES AND SCHOOLS

1. Become efficient in your use of time so you can find the time to train to be an effective advocate for your child.

2. Ask the Director of Special Education how you can volunteer to help her with projects. Find a way that you can work with him/her to make the school a better place for all kids.

When I moved into my town, I wrote the SPED director a letter introducing myself and asking her if my skills would be of any value to her. I advised her that I was available for projects and committees. I was very clear as to what my vision was, full and successful inclusion for all students with disabilities. I included a business card, which just had everyone's name in my family and our contact information. When I went to see the SPED director for the first time, I noticed that my card was tacked onto her small and private bulletin board. I have remained true to my promise. I have volunteered for every possible opportunity. I have approached her with ideas for the school district and offered to do all of the work. I have rescheduled doctor appointments and even vacations just to accommodate her wishes. If I did not agree with or respect the SPED director, I would still go out of my way to get on her good side, without compromising my values or philosophy. Fortunately, in my district, I discovered an extremely intelligent and caring individual who was committed to

following both the law and best educational practices
in our school district.
~Anne Treimanis

3. Start or join a parent group. Make sure there are networking opportunities as well as informational speakers. Create a website for your parent group so parents know where to go for information. Or create a Facebook page for the group. But be aware that the school district will probably monitor the Facebook page. Think about which privacy settings work best for your group. Don't be surprised that they are looking – heck, I always check out the Facebook pages of school board attorneys or administrators.

4. Educate the staff about your child's disability and about your child's needs. Sometimes it appears that the school is refusing to meet your child's needs. In fact, they just don't understand what is needed. You must teach them what you know, based on your unique and rich journey as a parent of a child with a disability.

5. Don't view the school as an enemy. Understand that most teachers want to include your child, they just may not know how. Professor Lou Brown says, *"Water professionals and they will grow."* I have found that given the opportunity, professionals will rise to the occasion.

6. Family participation in school activities promotes a feeling of school community and solidarity between schools and families.

7. Write thank you letters. Don't wait until the last day; write them all year long. When a teacher makes extraordinary efforts to include your child, thank them in a letter with a copy to the principal so the letter will go into the personnel file. Let the administration know when staff is doing a good job. Most people respond positively to praise and will work harder and smarter as a result. Thank you letters can also be used as a way to document conversations, but usually should not have a hidden agenda.

8. Find many ways to give positive feedback. If a teacher does something to facilitate an inclusive school community, write a press release and send it to the local newspaper. Then make copies of the article and send it to the teacher, as well as the principal. Ask that the story be put in the teacher's file.

9. When you form alliances with school staff, don't forget employees who are not teachers or administrators. It is important to have good relationships with the cafeteria staff, the secretaries, the custodians, the nurse, and the playground and bus supervisors. They work hard and they deserve your respect. These people are invaluable to help your child be fully and successfully included. They can make the school a more pleasant and friendly place. They can also be your eyes and ears when you are not in school. Ask them for their opinions; they see everything. Make sure you remember to thank them for their care and services. Notice them, do nice things for them throughout the year.

One time a custodian walked over to me and said how wonderful it was that Ieva was going to classes with all the other kids and how different it was when he was a child. He then went on to say that Ieva had been happy at the school the last couple of years and that's why he was surprised to find her hiding in his supply closet lately! As it turns out, there were some issues brewing at school that only came to my attention via the custodian.

Another time a mother called the school to report that my daughter was picking her nose on the bus and should not be allowed to ride. The school toyed around with some rules that Ieva would have to follow if she wanted to keep her riding privileges. It was the bus driver who intervened and said that most of the kids picked their noses, even more so than Ieva and also my daughter was one of the few students who sat safely in her seat.

Since middle school, the cashier in the cafeteria has been a godsend. I can count on my child being warmly greeted every day. When I occasionally drop in for lunch, I learn who has been helpful during lunch and who my daughter sits with.

The stories go on and on, each and every year. I am forever indebted to the band of hard working individuals who answer the phones and clean the schools and serve the lunches at school.

~Anne Treimanis

TIPS ON BULLYING

1. Try to build resiliency in your child so that h/she is less likely to get hurt if s/he is bullied. Some ways to build resiliency are:
   - Spend time together as a family. Do activities together. Eat meals together.
   - Encourage positive relationships with positive adult role models outside the immediate family.
   - Make sure your child has hobbies (sports, music, art, clubs). Those interests can serve as a buffer to negative influences.
   - Encourage community service. This also serves as a buffer to negative peer behavior.
   - Teach self calming strategies.
   - Teach problem-solving skills.

2. If your child has been bullied, here is what you can consider doing...
   - Help your child decide how serious the incident was, but always take bullying seriously.
   - Try to stay calm so your child talks to you.
   - Keep a log of all events. Document everything that happens.
   - Talk to the teacher or the principal.

- Consider calling the police. Sometimes the bullying stops the day you call the cops.
- Is there a bullying law in your state? If so, learn it. Find out what the bullying policies in your school are and see if the school is following the rules.
- If your child is suffering from bullying, get them professional mental health counseling.
- Let the school know, in writing, that you are beginning this therapy as a result of the bullying, so you preserve later claims.
- Consider speaking to the parents of the bully, although those conversations are not always welcomed.

3. If your child is mistreating others, consider the following:
   - Is h/she imitating characters on TV, the movies, or a video game?
   - Does h/she think it is funny?
   - Does h/she have his/her own anger issues?
   - Does h/she need training in interpersonal skills?
   - Does h/she retaliate against the victim, and if so, why?
   - Does h/she need professional mental health counseling?

4. If your child has witnessed bullying, consider the following:
   - Encourage him/her to spend time supporting the victim.
   - Encourage him/her to speak to a trusted adult about it.
   - Encourage him/her to report what h/she has seen.

5. If you are concerned about bullying, check out the resources on http://www.stopbullying.gov.

6. Check out these great tips from Special Education Advocate Gerri Fleming:

- TIP: Often schools will try to get the bully and the victim to make amends. THIS IS A TERRIBLE IDEA. Do not allow this. The power differential still exists between the bully and the victim. It only gives the bully a chance to shine in front of school officials and it may result in retaliation that moves "underground." Also, if this request is made by school personnel, it indicates a poor understanding on their part, of the problems associated with bullying. Ask the school to get technical assistance from experts in the field.

- TIP: If there is any talk of removal from a class or program—make sure the victim is not the recipient of the removal, as this can happen. It sends a stronger message to the victim, the bully and the student body, if the victim remains in the class and the bully is removed, that bullying has real-life consequences and will not be tolerated.

- TIP: Do not neglect to consider law enforcement involvement. In some cases, it may be warranted.

- TIP: If bullying occurs on the bus, ask for the bully to be removed—suspended or expelled--from the bus. Student transportation is not a right, but a privilege. Tax dollars should not be used on those who harass others in protected classes. More often than not, the parent of the victim removes his/her child from the bus and transports the child with a disability to and from school.

This amounts to further victimization of the family by the bully.

- TIP: If school personnel contributed to the bullying through neglect or active participation, consider sending a complaint to your State Department of Education filing for the revocation of that person's certification/license.
- TIP: When children with disabilities are bullied because of their disability, it rises to the standard of "disability harassment." Children with disabilities are a protected class. If your child is harassed/bullied because of his/her disability, you must notify the school by letter. There are elements that must be included in this letter, named for a particular court case, Gebser v. Lago Vista Independent School District. See Appendix 13 Gebser Notice Template.

TIPS ON FRIENDSHIPS

1. The two keys to friendship are close proximity and frequent opportunity to interact. Therefore, make sure your child has close proximity to peers by attending typical classes in your neighborhood school. There is where frequent opportunity to interact will occur.

2. Again, always consider close proximity and frequent opportunity to interact. Enroll your child in typical community activities. If your child needs support, ask that those supports be put into place.

3. Friendships can be better fostered if the teacher uses cooperative learning strategies. Your child can and should be a meaningful member of cooperative groups in school. If kids are pitted against each other in highly competitive activities, then friendship opportunities are lost. When students work together in school, it builds a stronger foundation for developing friendships.

4. The teachers can be key in fostering friendships. They are role models for the other students. They must value each child with or without a disability and respect learning differences. If you notice that the adults in school treat your child in a condescending manner or in a way that is not age-appropriate, ask them to stop:

> *I attended an IEP meeting with a friend. She shared that recently her young daughter with Down syndrome had a play-date. A small squabble occurred, and the visiting friend said, "If you don't play nicely with me, you won't get your Hershey Kiss as a reward." How telling this was, the young friend was imitating how she saw the teacher treat the student at school. Children notice everything.*
> *~Anne Treimanis*

5. Encourage the teachers to find ways to highlight your child's strengths, interests, and talents. If two kids love the same baseball team, board game, or they both fish, then there is an increased chance of friendship because they have something in common. Get acquainted activities are a great way to start off the school year. Ask the teacher how the other kids can get to know all about your child's hobbies, interests, and recent

vacations or adventures. If a child's hobby or area of expertise is celebrated in class, his/her status will be elevated in the eyes of his/her peers.

> One of the reasons we got a dog is so others kids would be attracted to our house, and my daughter would have something interesting to talk about. I selected an older dog that was well trained with good manners. I occasionally bring the dog with me when I have to pick up my daughter from an activity. Immediately, the other kids will swarm around us, wanting to pet the dog and asking questions about her. This gives my daughter a lot of positive attention.
> ~Anne Treimanis

6. Ask the teacher to infuse ability awareness training in the everyday curriculum. Provide the teachers lists of accomplishments that persons with disabilities have contributed to our society. These lists are readily available on the internet. Make sure that social justice is part of what kids are learning. Visit the classroom and talk about civil rights.

7. Ask the teachers which kids seem to be interested and friendly with your child. Then find a way to extend this interest to after school hours. Invite them over or plan an interesting activity and invite them to join you.

8. It's hard to have friends when you can't communicate your ideas using words. Make sure your child has a way of communicating to others. Perhaps some form of assistive technology can give a student a way to communicate. Make sure his/her peers get trained in the technology, as well.

9. Some kids have too many adults surrounding them all day at school. These adults can be barriers to friendships. A teaching assistant should not be Velcroed onto your child or behave like a hovercraft. They are there to facilitate friendships, not to be your child's friend. Make sure that the teaching assistant understands this. In fact, tell him/her personally.

10. Consider discontinuing the use of a teaching assistant. Often they keep teachers from taking full ownership of the student. They enable the student to rely on someone else instead of becoming independent. Think about all the things that could happen without the assistance of a teaching assistance. Then see how natural supports could take the place of what the teaching assistant was doing. Dr. Michael Giangreco from the University of Vermont has done research in this area that you should become familiar with.

11. A child will not enjoy academic success if he/she is socially unhappy. Sometimes specific social skills can be taught. Meet with the school team and find out what skills your child might need and if those are skills that can formally be taught. Some skills include being pleasant, taking turns, smiling, giving compliments to others, being aware of personal space, and being interested in others. Remember, these skills do not have to be taught in isolation or in a group with other kids with disabilities. These skills can be part of a lunch bunch with typical peers.

12. Make sure your house has up-to-date fun and "cool" things to do, so kids will want to come over to visit. If you have the best toys or latest music, then your house will become a magnet for kids. Be sure that you offer tasty snacks or meals to guests and make them feel welcome. It's okay to get advice from other kids on what is the latest and greatest.

> *We bought Dance Dance Revolution and Karaoke when Ieva was a teenager. Our house grew five-fold in popularity!*
> *~Anne Treimanis*

13. Make sure your child dresses appropriately. It's okay to follow fashion fads. If a kid looks cool, other people may jump to the conclusion that h/she is cool. It's not fair to judge people by their outward appearances, but we do this all the time; make sure your child looks attractive and hip.

> *When my daughter Ieva had a growth spurt she needed new clothes. Frankly, I didn't know what was stylish so I asked Amy, a neighbor's daughter if she would help us shop. Amy was in the same grade as my daughter and was popular. We went off on a spree. Naturally I bought Amy a few articles of clothing! As a result, not only did we have a great time, but Ieva looked good, and Amy was eager to shop again or give us advice whenever we needed new clothes.*
> *~Anne Treimanis*

BACK-TO-SCHOOL TIPS FOR THE FIRST DAY OF SCHOOL

1. Get excited about the big day! Talk about it every day, mark the day on the calendar. Make a special trip to the store with your child to buy school supplies. Consider getting a new backpack or some new back-to-school clothes.

2. Think about transportation. Is it appropriate for your child? Remember that transportation is a related service and should be discussed at the IEP meetings. Are supports and services in place so that the transportation will work for your child?

3. Before the first day of school, try getting the children to sleep and then waking up in the morning at the same time your child will have to do so when school begins. Establish the sleep routine before school starts. If you are unsuccessful, then don't beat yourself up. Your child will be exhausted the first day, go to bed early that night, then the next day h/she will be up early.

4. If appropriate, your child should have met his/her new teachers ahead of time and visited the classroom. They should know where his/her locker is and how to open the lock. They should know where the water fountains are, the cafeteria, and the playground.

5. Give **each** teacher a copy of the IEP, or perhaps just a list of accommodations and services that they are expected to use. Include a photo of your child with the IEP.

6. Arrange for a private parent/teacher conference early in the year to discuss your child's unique personality.

1. Understand that IDEA 2004 requires IEP teams to consider the assistive technology needs of all children with disabilities. (20 U.S.C. 1414(d)(3)(B)(v)).

2. It's not okay for the school to check a box in the IEP form that says "assistive technology has been considered but is not required," when no conversation has taken place during the meeting.

3. Understand that IDEA 2004 defines an 'assistive technology device' as "any item, piece of equipment, or product system, whether acquired commercially off the shelf, modified, or customized, that is used to increase, maintain, or improve functional capabilities of a child with a disability. (20 U.S.C. 1401(1)).

4. Understand that IDEA 2004 defines an 'assistive technology service' as "any service that directly assists a child with a disability in the selection, acquisition, or use of an assistive technology device. Such term includes -
"(A) the evaluation...
(B) purchasing, leasing, or otherwise providing for the acquisition of assistive technology devices...

(C) selecting, designing, fitting, customizing, adapting, applying, maintaining, repairing, or replacing...

(D) coordinating and using other therapies, interventions, or services with assistive technology devices...

(E) training or technical assistance for such child, or ...the family of such child...

(F) training or technical assistance for professionals... (20 U.S.C. 1401(2))"

5. In other words, it's not just access to computers. Ask the team if Assistive Technology, high, mid, or low tech, can give the student more meaningful access to the general education curriculum.

6. Consider working with the school to lock down the computers and tablets so students do not get in trouble for search history and inappropriate internet use.

7. Understand that IDEA 2004 requires schools to provide assistive technology training for the teachers, child, and family. (20 U.S.C. 1400(2)(E) & (F)).

8. Parents should be trained in the assistive technology that their children are using and that technology should go home. Teachers should know how to use the technology that the IEP team recommends; otherwise it will sit in the shelf.

1. Think about school-wide positive behavior supports, not just an individualized plan. Check https://www.pbis.org/school for more information.

2. Request that a functional behavior assessment (FBA) of your child's behavior be conducted and the results shared with you prior to the IEP meeting.

3. Discuss the FBA at the IEP meeting. Find out what were the ABCs: what happens before the behavior (Antecedent), what the behavior actually looks like (Behavior), and what were the consequences or reward (Consequences).

4. Ask the evaluator and the entire team if they have a hypothesis as to why the behavior is occurring.

5. Find out what the rest of the class and the responsible adults were doing when the behaviors occurred. For example, the student may have been bored because the lesson was not modified to their level and the resulting behavior helped him/her escape by having to go to the Principal's office. Or maybe everyone was bored but the typical students could hide their cell phones as they were texting and only the student with an IEP did not have that skill, and got caught.

6. Inquire about behaviors across all settings, including home, and try to determine what might account for the differences.

7. Discuss rewards. Don't let the school give your child candy or junky food. One in three children in the United States are overweight and your child doesn't need to join the ranks. It also encourages emotional eating.

8. When you write behavior goals, use measurable, and clear descriptions of behaviors. Don't use descriptors like angry or frustrated. Instead use what can be seen such as throwing books, kicking with feet, laying on floor, jumping up and down, and/or screaming.

9. Consider writing goals not only for decreasing the problem behavior, but also for increasing positive behavior.

ADDRESSING EXECUTIVE FUNCTION CONCERNS

1. Many schools like to write accommodations for executive function concerns, but not teach executive function skills. Make sure your child is taught strategies to address Executive Function issues.

2. Teach skills, but also rely on technology. Students with executive functioning issues should be using Google Calendar or iCal. They also need productivity apps and apps that keep them healthy.

TREIMANIS' STRATEGIES FOR "SHARPENING THE SAW"

1. Read Steve Covey's book, The 7 Habits of Highly Effective People. Habit #7 is How to Sharpen the Saw.

2. I always buy CDs from conferences that help me understand inclusion, the law, or have advocacy instruction. I play these recordings, sometimes over and over whenever I am driving somewhere, so traveling by car becomes a time to be empowered. Try to upgrade your car stereo so it has the capability to play MP3 format. In this way, several hours of seminars, sometimes the entire conference, can be played from just one MP3 CD. It's less expensive to buy conference CDs this way. These days there is often an option to download the conference seminars from a website, then play them from your iPhone or iPod through your car stereo system. If you can't figure it out, ask your car dealer or almost any teenager to assist you.

3. I'm not the only one who likes to learn in the car. Zig Ziglar suggests you should turn your car into a rolling university.

4. I upload my CDs to iTunes and then make sure several are in my iPod or iPhone, and play them while doing some tedious or automatic duties, such as grocery shopping. Sometimes, if I am watching my children play in the distance, such as sitting on a park bench while they are on the playground equipment, I'll start listening to an empowering talk. It's better than reading a book if you need to keep your eyes on your children. Also, if another Mom sits next to me and starts idle chatter, merely to pass away the time, I simply say, "Sorry to be rude but I am taking a class and I need to hear this lecture before our test this week."

5. When a good speaker is presenting, I bring a digital recorder to their seminar. I then listen to the recording, sometimes over and over and over. When you hear an excellent presentation several times, the knowledge stays with you. Also, if there are good "one-liners" and "comebacks," I incorporate that into my personal repertoire.

6. I purchase or borrow DVDs on disability related topics and watch them while walking on the treadmill. I purchase new DVDs, win them on E-bay, or borrow them from local disability related organizations.

7. In addition to the DVDs, I find disability related YouTube videos and watch them on my iPad while I am walking on my treadmill. The more I walk, the more I learn about advocacy. Also, the more I walk, the greater my energy is to keep battling for justice.

8. When you think of a good idea, write it quickly in your phone, iPad, on your computer, or in a notepad. Have a folder created for good ideas or tips. If that idea comes to you while in the car, have a tiny recorder always handy to speak into. Get familiar with the recording apps on your phone and iPad. I use the Evernote app for my ideas.

9. I keep books on inclusion on my bathroom counter where I blow dry and curl my hair. I can read while curling. Since the books are so interesting, I give my hair plenty of time to be curled so I not only look good for the day but also I am well-

informed. I also keep important books next to my bed, so I can read if I can't sleep.

10. I print important parts of the law on index cards and place them on the mirror and cupboards so they can painlessly be committed to memory.

11. Recently, I changed my lifestyle to include walking on the treadmill every morning and eating very healthy mostly organic foods. I have more energy to advocate for my clients and my daughter. My mind is clearer and I can work more effectively. For the curious, I get most of my nutritional advice from Dr. Mark Hyman's books.

TIPS ON ORGANIZING PARENT GROUPS

1. If your town doesn't have a special education parent group, then start one!

2. Decide if you want to just have an informal handful of like-minded folks to make changes in your town or if you want a big formal organization with by-laws.

3. Consider partnering with your school district. The Director of Special Education can reach every family who has a child receiving special education services to help your group. The district can also provide free meeting space in the school. Some groups become part of the PTA (Parent Teacher Association). Often you have shared goals.

4. Sometimes formal partnerships with the district can cramp your style. If you need to be independent, consider forming a Not-for-Profit group, and take the extra step of being recognized by the IRS as such, by becoming a 501(c)(3) organization. Perks include being eligible to apply for grants, being able to accept donations that are tax-deductible for the donors, and not paying taxes when you shop. If you are an official 501(c)(3) organization, you can get fabulous discounts on software from http://www.techsoup.org.

5. Be organized. Put all of your information in a file. Or keep good electronic files. If you are working with a few folks, consider putting all your documents (email lists, flyers, thank you letters, legal papers, and everything else) on a free Dropbox account at http://dropbox.com. The folks helping you will all have access to Dropbox.

6. Put together a website or a Facebook page for your group.

7. Run informational seminars with guest speakers. Make sure you know how to get the publicity out (school announcements, newspapers both paper and online, listservs, and community bulletin boards). When running meetings, consider partnering with other groups. They can help with manpower, publicity, and refreshments.

8. Find good meeting spaces. Think about community spaces, restaurants, and spaces in agency headquarters.

9. Try to organize several meetings at a time, even the platform for the entire year. Calendars fill up fast and your potential participants should be able to protect the dates you choose.

10. When putting together publicity, use People First Language. See https://www.disabilityisnatural.com for language guidance.

11. Never forget the three F's of a good meeting – free, fun, and food.

12. Check out this comprehensive free publication, "Organizing Parents: Building Family Advocacy Organizations" from the State of Connecticut Office of Protection and Advocacy for Persons with Disabilities at http://www.ct.gov/opapd/lib/opapd/documents/adobe/organizing_parents.pdf.

13. Read what Sue Whitney, Research Editor at Wrightslaw has to say about forming a parent group at http://www.wrightslaw.com/heath/advo.group.org.htm.
Especially amusing but true is her take on how parents are perceived when they form a group in a district that is not parent-friendly...

    1 person = A fruitcake

    2 people = A fruitcake and a friend

    3 people = Troublemakers

    5 people = "Let's have a meeting"

    10 people = "We'd better listen"

    25 people = "Our dear friends"

50 people = "A powerful organization"

14. Bring Pete and Pam Wright to your district for a boot camp to train parents on their rights. Find out how to bring the Wrights to your town at http://www.wrightslaw.com.

OTHER LAWS

1. Educate yourself about other laws that protect students with disabilities.

2. Become familiar with your state's bullying statute – if they have one. To learn more about bullying, check out http://www.stopbullying.gov. Your State Department of Education should have someone who will take formal complaints on bullying.

3. Become familiar with Title IX of the Education Amendments of 1972, which protects students from sexual harassment and gender discrimination. Title IX protects people from discrimination based on sex in education programs or activities that receive Federal financial assistance. Your State Department of Education should have a Title IX Coordinator. Title IX states that: *"No person in the United States shall, on the basis of sex, be excluded from participation in, be denied the benefits of, or be subjected to discrimination under any education program or activity receiving Federal financial assistance."*

4. Become familiar with the McKinney Veto Homeless Assistance Act (42 U.S.C. 11431 et seq.) which protects students who are homeless. Here is the law's Statement of Policy.

"The following is the policy of the Congress:

(1) Each State educational agency shall ensure that each child of a homeless individual and each homeless youth has equal access to the same free, appropriate public education, including a public preschool education, as provided to other children and youths.

(2) In any State that has a compulsory residency requirement as a component of the State's compulsory school attendance laws or other laws, regulations, practices, or policies that may act as a barrier to the enrollment, attendance, or success in school of homeless children and youths, the State will review and undertake steps to revise such laws, regulations, practices, or policies to ensure that homeless children and youths are afforded the same free, appropriate public education as provided to other children and youths.

(3) Homelessness alone is not sufficient reason to separate students from the mainstream school environment.

(4) Homeless children and youths should have access to the education and other services that such children and youths need to ensure that such children and youths have an opportunity to meet the same challenging State student academic achievement standards to which all students are held".

5. Learn about Guardianship and Conservatorship. But at the end of the day, do NOT go to court to get control over your child; it is undignified and dangerous. You can accomplish your goals in other ways, most notably by using a Durable Power of Attorney.

6. Find out if your child can get benefits through the Social Security Administration. Children with disabilities who meet income requirements may be eligible for Supplemental Security Income SSI. Adults with Disabilities with limited income and resources may also be eligible for these benefits. This also results in eligibility for Medicare benefits. If a parent has a disability or is 65 or older, there may be an opportunity for the child with a disability to collect under SSDI—Social Security Disability Insurance. The amount may be more than SSI. Contact SSA for more information. http://www.ssa.gov. Make sure your child gets an IQ test BEOFRE age 18 with accompanying adaptive scales in order to get certain benefits for individuals with intellectual disabilities.

7. Become familiar with the Freedom of Information Act (FOIA) in your state. Sometimes this is known as the Freedom of Information Law (FOIL). FOIA gives individuals the right to get copies of government agency documents, including complaints against a school, letters, contracts, information on how much the school board attorneys get paid, etc. See Appendix 14 for sample FOIA letter.

8. Become familiar with Section 504 of the Rehabilitation Act of 1973, which protects students with disabilities who need accommodations to level the playing field. Section 504 follows students to college, where IDEA does not. Section 504 is a federal law designed to protect the rights of individuals with disabilities in programs and activities that receive Federal financial assistance from the U.S. Department of Education. Section 504 provides: *"No otherwise qualified individual with a disability in the United States . . . shall, solely by reason of her or his disability, be excluded from the participation in, be denied the benefits of, or be subjected to discrimination under any program or activity receiving Federal financial assistance . . . ."*

9. Become familiar with the Americans with Disabilities Act. The ADA prohibits discrimination on the basis of disability in employment, State and local government, public accommodations, commercial facilities, transportation, and telecommunications. To be protected by the ADA, one must have a disability or have a relationship or association with an individual with a disability. An individual with a disability is defined by the ADA as a person who has a physical or mental impairment that substantially limits one or more major life activities, a person who has a history or record of such an impairment, or a person who is perceived by others as having such an impairment. Here is a good starting point to learn about this law at http://www.ada.gov.

THE PARENT SIDE ©™

ONE MINUTE   THE NEXT   AND THEN WHAT?...

Cartoon courtesy of Colleen Tomko. http://www.kidstogether.org
Please shop for her disability-themed gifts at:
http://www.cafepress.com/theparentside

1. Sometimes these tips do not work on their own. Then it's time to look for other solutions.

2. You must thoroughly understand your procedural safeguards. You have so many rights: Don't be the parent who is unaware of what h/she is entitled to.

3. Start with handling disagreements in a diplomatic manner. When that does not work, on rare occasions, the circumstances might call for taking steps to see if the educators should lose their certification to teach. Check with your State Department of Education to see how that's done.

4. In some instances, you can bring your case to the public, using the press, instead of choosing to exercise your procedural rights.

5. When educators are negligent and they cause harm to your children, you might have a case for a personal injury attorney who specializes in negligence. Most negligence attorneys work on a percentage basis which is statutorily controlled. In other words, the attorney gets one-third of what h/she recovers.

6. If you bring a law suit against the District for negligence and later, separately, negotiate a settlement for an appropriate education, make sure you do not lose your rights under the concurrent negligence suit.

7. Sometimes when educators hurt children you should consider calling the Department of Children and Families to report them. This Child Welfare agency has different names in each state.

TIPS TO PREPARE FOR MEDIATION

These are the tips I give my clients in Connecticut. Find out what the differences might be in your state. If you cannot resolve your differences at the IEP meeting, consider going to mediation.

1. Bring the student's file. But more importantly, make sure it is organized to the point where you pull out quickly whatever it is that you are looking for. When you fumble for papers, it's distracting and an inefficient use of time. Try to predict what you will need and have it handy.

2. Court room appearance is not necessary, but don't be too casually dressed.

3. Bring water, food, and snacks. In the worst case scenario, you might be trapped in a room until 6pm with no refreshments and there will not be a lunch break. Some districts will provide coffee, water, and a few snacks, but you cannot count on this. Most mediations end by 4PM at the latest. The mediator may leave us for a few minutes and return, or 2 hours and return - as h/she goes back and forth between rooms. There is no way to predict when h/she returns so we need to always stay put.

4. Bring something to share with the mediator and often they are thrilled to accept. But they don't want to feel like they are taking "your stuff." So, if you have ice tea, then you must have 3 bottles so it's clear to see that there is extra. Or if you have snacks, there must be a large amount so it's clear you couldn't possibly eat that much.

5. Bring copies of any invoices that you hope to get reimbursed for. If there are several expenses, write them all out on a spread sheet.

6. Bring a real calculator; do not depend on the calculator feature of your iPhone. Bring pens and pads of paper.

7. The mediator may begin by having the parties together and allowing each side to give an opening statement. If h/she doesn't want an opening statement, h/she might ask to simply state the issues, and then ask the other side to restate what they heard. Then h/she will separate the Board and the family into different rooms. Or h/she may keep you separate from the very beginning. You need to be prepared for each scenario.

8. Mediation depends not only on the law, but on relationships. While you do not have to compromise the student's rights, you need to remain positive, professional, and pleasant.

9. The mediator will need help staying on top of facts, as will the Board and the student's team. The family has been living the case day and night, and all the facts and issues are ready to spill

out. But everyone else in the room is a professional with other clients. While we expect that the professionals will be fully prepared, it's helpful to have a list of key points at your fingertips. Each mediator comes to the table with different levels of skill and different levels of preparation. In the past, I have prepared outlines of the issues, timelines, or lists of facts for the mediator and offered to give it to him/her if h/she wants to accept it. Usually the mediators are appreciative.

10. Bring a laptop or iPad in case you want to quickly research something. My laptop and iPad have a Verizon card in it and it works wherever there is cell service.

11. Make sure that you don't have appointments or childcare issues so you do not have to worry and stare at the clock. But do wear a watch in case there is no clock in the room and you are wondering about the time.

12. Bring Tylenol or Advil or whatever you need for headaches and stress. Stay hydrated.

APPENDIX 1 – REQUEST FOR RECORDS

October 9, 2015

Mr. Sigmund Freud, School Psychologist
Happytown High School
56 Elm Street
Happytown, CT 06840

Re: FERPA Request for all of Eva Smith's records

Dear Mr. Freud,

In preparation for Eva's upcoming IEP meeting, I am requesting a copy of all of Eva's records since September 1, 2005. I am entitled to these records under FERPA, The Family Education Rights and Privacy Act, and IDEA, The Individuals With Disabilities Education Act, and state statute.

Please include all of her records, WHICH INCLUDE BUT ARE NOT LIMITED TO: her cumulative file, her confidential file, and her compliance file. Please include all reports written as a result of the school's evaluations; reports of independent evaluations; medical records; summary reports of evaluation team and eligibility committee meetings; IEP's; any correspondence retained between myself and the school officials; any correspondence written between school personnel regarding my daughter including emails; any records maintained by the school nurse, Eva's teachers, and any member of the IEP team; notes or letters written in connection with any planning or discussions, or any other matters in connection with my daughter Eva Smith. Please include any and all personally identifiable information that exists.

Thanks in advance for your cooperation.

Very truly yours,

Anne Smith
Full Contact Info

Parent Concerns
Eva Smith IEP / May 16, 2016
Submitted by Anne and John Smith
(please attach to the IEP)

1. Safety:
Eva is not safe at school. Her behavior plan is routinely disregarded.
Suggested Resolution: Staff must be familiar with the behavior plan and they must have the ability to follow it. Technical assistance is required for staff.

2. Behavior Plan:
The behavior plan is not being followed. For example, the plan states that if there is an instance of tantrums, the staff will disengage Eva (not verbally attempt to redirect her, remove eye contact). Instead, the staff keeps asking her questions such as, "What's the matter?" "Is something bothering you?"

3. FAPE (Free Appropriate Public Education):
Eva's IEP is routinely disregarded.
Suggested Resolution: We are asking that an appropriate program is put into place. We are also requesting compensatory education for lack of FAPE since September 2015.

4. Reading:
Eva is reading several years behind grade level. Her current program, Edmark, is not research or evidence based. She needs a comprehensive diagnostic reading evaluation by a reading specialist to determine what scientific peer-reviewed multi-sensory reading program she needs so she can become a proficient reader. Her only reading evaluation, conducted 5 years ago, was done by a Highly Qualified Special Education Teacher, who has NO background in reading, and all she did was the reading subtests of the Woodcock Johnson IV.

5. LRE (Least Restrictive Environment):

Eva needs supports, supplemental aides and services in order to be successful in the general education classroom. Instead of discussing what supports and services would be appropriate, the District chose to remove Eva to a more restrictive environment.

Suggested Resolution: Return Eva to the general education classroom without delay with the supports she is entitled to.

6. Sensory Issues:

Eva is a student with significant sensory issues. Yet her sensory needs are being ignored.

Suggested Resolution: We are requesting a sensory integration evaluation to find out how sensory needs are interfering with access to the general education curriculum and proactive strategies need to be put into place.

7. OT (Occupational Therapy):

Eva's handwriting and drawing skills are poor which indicate continued need for OT.

8. Bullying:

Eva has been bullied by other students. On one occasion, on January 17, Eva ran away from a bully who called her the "R" word and then pushed her into the bushes.

9. Discrimination against Eva due to her disability:

Assistant Director of Special Education, Jason Rachet, is enforcing a policy that no child is permitted to play with Eva unless written permission is received from that student's parents. This policy is not in place for students without disabilities.

10. Humiliation:

Eva is humiliated in several ways, including but not limited to the following:

a. Principal Silva yells at Eva in front of staff. This is not only humiliating, but a clear violation of the behavior plan.

b. Principal Silva announced to Eva's class, on February 2, that if they saw Eva in school, not to worry, she was not dangerous.

11. Suspensions:
Eva has been suspended from school due to the failure of the District to follow the IEP. In addition, Eva is sent home early from school, which are defacto suspensions, and no suspension reports are written for these days.

12. Goals:
After reviewing all of the goals for next year, it was determined that some are not measurable. Establishing concrete criteria for measuring progress toward the attainment of each goal is crucial to Eva's success. We will go over these during the IEP meeting.

13. Self-Advocacy:
Eva needs help with self-advocacy in the following areas:
a. Communicating when she does not understand an assignment or concept in class.
b. Communicating her need for help and reporting bullying episodes to adults.
c. Eva needs help to know what to say to peers who bully or tease her. Eva can easily be set up by other kids to take a dare and needs help in those situations.

14. Parents are not meaningful members of the IEP team:
The parents were not given the Behavior Incident Forms as they were generated. Their input at IEP meetings is disregarded. Decisions are made prior to the IEP meeting.

January 8, 2016
Ms. Kara Pocono, Special Education Administrator
Happytown School
456 Elm Street
Happytown, CT 06840

Letter sent via email attachment and also sent via first class mail

Dear Ms. Pocono,

Thank you for your telephone call yesterday, January 7. You told me that my daughter's transcript was going to be changed from Biology to Biology Survey. She would continue to be in the exact same class doing the exact same modified work, but the name of the class for her alone would be changed. You mentioned that the teacher did not feel it was fair to continue to give her B grades when in fact, her B was so very different that the B grades that the typical students earned. I stated that I was not willing to have the name of the class changed because it was a discriminatory act.

You also advised me that due to the Speech and Language Pathologist going out on maternity leave, my daughter's speech services would drop from 2 times weekly to once a week, as all students with IEPs would have to share the remaining SLP. I advised you that Eva's services needed to reflect her needs, not staffing issues. I stated that the level of service would have to remain the same, unless you offered to pay for outside services.

If this is not your recollection of our conversation, please advise me in writing within the next 5 days. Thanks very much.

Very truly yours,

Anne Smith
123 Main Street / Happytown, CT 06840
Tel: (203) 966-1234 / Fax: (203) 966-5678
Smith99@ail.com

Your Name
Street Address
City, State, Zip Code
Daytime telephone number and email

Today's Date (include month, day, and year)

Name of school staff on the IEP Team (case manager or person who seems to be in charge)
Name of School
Street Address
City, State, Zip Code

Re: Jane Doe IEP Meeting on March xx, 2016

Dear (name),

In preparation for my child's upcoming IEP meeting, I would like a copy of the draft IEP, all proposed Goals and Objectives, teacher reports, evaluations that you will be discussing or relying on, and any documents whatsoever that you will be using to prepare for the IEP. I need these documents in order to be a meaningful member of the IEP team. Please have these available five days before the meeting. You can email them to me at xxx@gmail.com or fax me at 203-567-1234. Thanks very much.

Sincerely,

Your name

Parent Concerns for_____ **Date:**_____
PLEASE ATTACH THIS TO THE IEP

Academic/Cognitive: Language Arts: (reading, writing, spelling)
Strengths (include data as appropriate):
Concerns (or needs):
Impact (to involvement and progress in the general education curriculum):

Academic/Cognitive: Math:
Strengths:
Concerns:
Impact:

Other Academic/Nonacademic Areas: (Science, Social Studies, Electives, Gym, Art, Music, etc...)
Strengths:
Concerns:
Impact:

Social/Emotional/Behavior:
Strengths:
Concerns:
Impact:

Communication:
Strengths:
Concerns:
Impact:

Vocational/Transition:
Strengths:
Concerns:
Impact:

Health and Development-Vision and Hearing: (list all diagnoses here under Concerns)
Strengths:
Concerns:
Impact:

Fine Motor:
Strengths:
Concerns:
Impact:

Gross Motor:
Strengths:
Concerns:
Impact:

Activities of Daily Living:
Strengths:
Concerns:
Impact:

APPENDIX 6 - PROPOSAL MATRIX

Proposal /Request	No - Why not?	Yes – Who implements? Who Oversees? Qualifications?	When - Start date? Frequency? Duration? Length of session? What does student miss?	Where/How Many - setting? Who are the others in group? # of kids in group? Needs of others in group?
Attendees				

Courtesy of Special Education Advocate Gerri Fleming
http://www.ctadvocacy.com

These statements are often overheard at IEP meetings (with occasional exaggeration) and my suggested responses...

School: You're recording this IEP meeting?? I thought we had a trusting relationship. Fine, then now we have to take our recorder out

Parent: I do place a lot of trust in the school. I want to record the meeting so I make sure I hear everything, so I don't misunderstand anything and I have an accurate record to help me.

****

School: We need to hurry since we only have 30 minutes scheduled for this IEP.

Parent: I have no intention to be rushed. If we do not finish this meeting we will have to reschedule.

****

Parent: Jimmy is still not decoding on grade level. I would like him have reading instruction by a highly qualified reading specialist one period each day. As you know, my independent reading evaluator said he needed daily reading instruction, either one to one or in a small group with closely matched peers. My evaluator said that my son needed an evidenced based scientific peer-reviewed reading program that was Orton-Gillingham based.

School: Don't worry, we have a highly qualified special education teacher who will meet your son's needs in the resource room. The special education teacher has experience using the Edmark program. Besides, your son has an intellectual disability. You can't expect him to read as well as the other kids. But don't worry, the Edmark program teaches you how to recognize the most common words.

Parent: But Edmark is not an evidenced based reading program. It doesn't address the 5 areas of reading identified by the National Reading Panel. And memorizing more words is not what my son needs, he needs to learn how to decode.

****

Parent: The special education teacher has no background in reading and should not be in charge of the reading goals.

School: What? She is a highly qualified special education teacher. In addition to giving the Edmark program to every student with Down syndrome that has ever been in our district, she's Wilson trained. That means she took a weekend class in how to use the Wilson materials. Furthermore, the reading specialists are reserved for the students with learning disabilities, while the students with ID and Autism get the special education teacher for their reading needs.

Parent: Some master level special education teachers have never taken course in reading.

****

School: How can you expect your child to read since he has an intellectual disability?

Parent: Decoding is not related to IQ, although I understand that comprehension is. I want my son to become a proficient decoder. Comprehension will be easier if he is not stumbling on what each word is.

****

Parent: Is this one of my child's teachers?

Psychologist: Oh no. Your child's teachers need to be in the classroom right now. As you know, IDEA has a new provision in which the entire team does not have to attend the IEP meetings. So, now we don't encourage them to attend. I will read the teacher's report.

Parent: But wait, don't you need my written consent if a team member is not here?

SPED teacher: I can run down the hall and grab the music teacher if the Mother is going to be difficult.

****

Psychologist: (reads form report) Jimmy is a delightful child with a mischievous grin. He is so well known in the school that we call him the Mayor of the High School. He has difficulty completing daily assignments and works 1:1 with a teaching assistant. In order to facilitate Jimmy's learning, we have placed his desk in the last row of the classroom so his teaching assistant can sit next to him. Jimmy has always been excused from taking the Common Core tests and naturally no student with ID would ever take the CAPT. Accordingly, we will excuse him from whatever assessments the new Smart Balance requires us to administer. Socially, Jimmy has had some difficulty relating to his classmates, but he is very kind to his teaching assistant. They always give each other the high five as they walk down the hall together. The teaching assistant loves having lunch with Jimmy every day. She's not like other paras, who ignore the students at lunch so they can sit and gab.

Parent: Um...excuse me for interrupting, but I really don't think it's appropriate for the teaching assistant to eat lunch every day with

Jimmy. Can't she help facilitate friendships between Jimmy and the other students?

Psychologist: The typical students have left Jimmy behind. The boys that Jimmy used to hang out with are now interested in girls and all the new high school activities. They don't have time to tolerate Jimmy anymore.

Speech Therapist: Your question leads me right into my speech report. Jimmy needs to develop his pragmatic language skills and improve his behavior before he can make new friends. He requires intensive speech language intervention in order to improve. In addition to pulling Jimmy out for direct therapy, I have decided to also put him in my social skills group so he can learn about good social skills, pragmatic skills, and how to interact with peers. It's during period E on Thursdays.

Parent: Isn't that during science?

Speech Therapist: Yes, but it's the only slot I have space in.

Parent: Who would be in this group with him? Would any of his friends from the middle school be there with him?

Speech Therapist: Oh no. We can't pull other students out of their academic classes. There will be other disabled children with IEP goals in the areas of socialization.

Parent: I am not sure this is the best way to meet Jimmy's social needs. What are pragmatic skills?

Principal: That just refers to how he is using his language.

Parent: Oh I see. Well, that is why we think he needs to be around his classmates so he can practice using language.

Principal: smiles and ignores mom's comment

Principal: I know you are concerned with his social experience. As students move from middle school to high school, the gap gets wider and it is less common for the regular education students to form friendships with disabled children. Don't you plan social activities for Jimmy outside of school?

****

SPED teacher: I don't know why you refuse to allow Jimmy to be a part of The Precious Pals program. The high school volunteers are very kind to the disabled kids. They go out for ice cream and they take them bowling.

Parent: I'd like to see Jimmy as a volunteer, but always being the person who is helped. Besides, there are 25 clubs here at the high school. Why are you steering us to Precious Pals?

Speech Therapist: I need to get back to students. Thanks, everyone. (Leaves)

Guidance Counselor: I need to leave also. I'm not really in charge of special education students. (Leaves)

****

School: We are not responsible for the progress your son makes.

Parent: The district is required to provide a program that is reasonably calculated to produce educational benefit. You also have to provide FAPE and monitor progress. If my son is not progressing, then let's talk about what supports he needs and what changes to the program we should make.

****

Psychologist: I'd like to give my report because I also need to leave soon. As you know, we have been very concerned about Jimmy's lack of academic progress and feel he would benefit from a more structured learning environment. Jimmy is not making progress in the mainstream and his behavior is becoming disruptive in class. He is telling us by his behavior that the general education environment is too much for him. In addition, I have analyzed his drawings and find that they are dominated by themes of abandonment and anxiety, as evidenced by this drawing of a tree. (holds up tree for everyone to see). We feel that he would benefit from a highly structured, low student-teacher ratio and a controlled learning environment where he can get the specialized instruction he needs.

Parent: My son is acting out because he is frustrated. Since he was very small, Jimmy has always reacted to frustration with the behaviors you are describing. My husband and I have found that if we break tasks down into smaller components, he learns much more quickly. Right now, there are no modifications to his classwork—he doesn't have the support he needs to complete his work. And Jimmy told us that it was very embarrassing to be in the back of the room doing simple worksheets with the teaching assistant on Tuesday when the rest of the class was working on a literature lesson.

Principal: Mrs. Smith, Jimmy is only reading at the fourth grade level...

Parent: Well, couldn't Jimmy have the stories the class is reviewing on audiotape so he can listen as the other students are doing silent reading? And when the class is reviewing the book, Jimmy could have the text in his hands to follow along. The teacher could use removable highlighting tape to emphasize the important parts of the story to keep Jimmy interested. Also, the book could be summarized and pre-taught to Jimmy so it would be easier for him to follow. Or, you could send the book home ahead of time, with audiotape, so Jimmy can listen to it the night before the lesson.

SPED Teacher: Maybe you could get a membership for The Library for the Blind and Disabled. But unfortunately, not all books are available on audiotape.

Parent: True, but I just recently read about software that's available that can actually read scanned text in a computerized voice back to the student, it's called Kurzweil.

Principal: That software wouldn't be practical. Computer lab is only once a week.

Parent: But Jimmy is supposed to have full time access to a computer – it says so in his IEP. We agreed that Jimmy would have a Chromebook available for every subject.

****

School: Your child is not making progress because she is never here. When you get her to school we can then educate her.

Parent: Please suggest supports and services that you will provide to my daughter so she is not so anxious to attend classes. If you are unable to do that, then we need to talk about a different placement.

****

Parent: Where is the iPad that the consultant recommended?

Principal: Yes, well, we are still looking into that. Our budget doesn't allow us to buy laptops and iPads for every student. And while everyone is begging for Kurzweil, it's too expensive. I am not going to ask the Board of Finance for more money so every single special education student can have that.

Parent: But we're not talking about every student, we are only talking about Jimmy and his individual needs. He needs to be taught in a way that takes his learning profile into account.

Principal: Listen lady. I wish I had an iPad with all those fancy apps. Plus, I could be sitting here playing Candy Crush Saga instead of paying attention to this conversation.

Parent: Well, when we attend YOUR IEP meeting we can discuss that. But right now we are sitting at Jimmy's PPT meeting so please let's focus on him.

****

Principal: I cannot expect each teacher to figure out the best way to teach your son in every single situation.

Parent: I'm not expecting that. This is a team effort. That's why I have requested that Jimmy's teachers have common planning time with the special education teacher. Jimmy's behavior wasn't an issue last year when he was properly supported and educational planning was being implemented on an ongoing basis. He was also a more active member of his class when he didn't feel so socially isolated.

Principal: In middle schools we have teams. But here in the high school we do not work in the team model. The special education is trying to meet with each teacher but it's very difficult.

Psychologist: Jimmy's socialization will be addressed in our social skills group for special needs students. In the meantime, I continue to be concerned with Jimmy's lack of academic progress. So, I have decided to perform the following evaluations. I can administer the WAIS, the Stamford-Binet, and a WISC III.

Principal: We really need to move forward. Have the new goals been read yet?

SPED Teacher: They will stay the same, only placement is different. By the way, IDEA says we don't need objectives anymore, so I just kept the general goals.

****

Parent: I really don't feel that the resource room is an appropriate placement for Jimmy. Can't we talk about modifying the curriculum? Maybe we could hire an educational consultant who has experience with inclusive education.

Principal: (Stands up, crosses arms) Excuse me. My staff has superior expertise in inclusive education. We've been doing it for years. I will not allow you to sit there and insult my staff.

SPED Teacher: The team feels that Jimmy should be in the resource room for academics and join the special needs social skills group to meet his social needs.

Parent: But I don't feel that way. I am a member of the IEP team.

SPED Teacher: That's true. But I meant the "school based team." Anyway, you are too personally and emotionally involved to make a reasonable decision.

Parent: Yes, I am very personally involved. That's precisely the reason I have a lot to contribute.

****

Principal: Look, if you really insist on general education, we can put Jimmy into a couple of the co-taught classes. We consider that general education.

Parent: Really? What percent of the students have IEPs in those classrooms?

Principal: About half. The other half have not been identified yet but should be. Luckily they have parents who are not savvy enough to advocate for services.

Parent: But 10% of all Students in this state have IEPs. If the co-taught classes contain students, half of whom have IEPs, you violate the law of natural proportions.

Principal: Okay, then forget my offer.

****

Psychologist: I plan to pull Jimmy out of the classroom on a weekly basis, on Tuesdays during period B, to discuss any issues that may be bothering him. If he has any frustrations, due to his home situation or whatever, he can find a safe haven in my office to share what's bothering him. I also think it would be a good idea to do projective personality testing to assess his mental state. Perhaps a psychiatric evaluation is warranted as well.

Parent: I will not consent to a psychiatric evaluation.

Psychologist: Hmmmm. I see now where Jimmy gets his anger issues from. I am going to put your statement in the file we are secretly keeping on you.

Parent: Secret files? I did not see any files on me when I gave sent you a FERPA request and got a full copy of my son's records, which is any record that is personally identifiable to him.

Principal: All incriminating records are weeded out before we send them to the parents. We do keep them though, in case we need them for due process.

****

School: Your child simply can't behave. Why don't you put him on meds?

Parent: Schools are prohibited from advising parents to medicate their children. School attendance cannot be based on that. If behavior impedes my child's learning, or the learning of others, you are required to put in place supports and services.

****

School: Billy is not telling us he is being bullied so there is nothing we can do about it.

Parent: Am I to understand that a bullying investigation only takes place when the child reports it? My child is trying to appear happy and stays quiet so no one sees how frightened he is. He has been having vivid nightmares since the bullying has become and often comes into our bed to sleep.

School: As a mandated reporter, I now have to call the Department of Children and Families to investigate why you are sharing a bed with your son.

****

School: I am sorry you didn't get your child's records in time for this IEP meeting. I was on maternity leave.

Parent: Without those records I am unable to be a meaningful participant in the IEP process. The school has an obligation to provide me with records on a timely basis when I request them.

****

SPED Teacher: It's just not possible to educate Jimmy only in a regular classroom. We also need to do whatever it takes to turn Jimmy back into a happy child. We love your son and we all want what's best for him.

Parent: What do you mean you love my son? You just met him three months ago! And I am not looking for what is best, I am looking for what is appropriate.

SPED Teacher: You really need to collaborate with us here. Truth be told, this team believes that Jimmy would benefit most from our brand new Life Skills Suite. It has a brand new kitchen in a simulated apartment. It's adjacent to the motor room and speech therapy room. The program includes field trips into the community where the kids learn to shop and bank. We know that Jimmy would do best in this program. But we understand you are still holding on to the inclusion dream. So that's why we are offering a combination of resource rooms for academics, and mainstream for lunch, gym, and music. We've already compromised for you, now please show us the same respect and compromise a little.

Principal: No one in this district is as committed to inclusion as I am. Please don't stand on your principles at the expense of your son's education. With some special help in the resource room, your son will make new friends with his own kind. Eventually he'll become a productive happy adult. Also, with intense one to one help, he'll eventually be ready to spend more time in the regular classroom.

Parent: My son shouldn't have to earn the right to be in a general education classroom. You are all speaking as though Jimmy has failed, but really, we have failed because it is our responsibility to provide him with the supports he needs to learn and progress in the general education curriculum.

SPED teacher: Mrs. Smith, let's not forget the fact that IDEA has never been fully funded.

Parent: I am tired of you always telling me about the fact that IDEA has never been fully funded. Let's start talking about the fact that IDEA has never been fully complied with!

Psychologist: You really should be grateful for the help we are offering. With all due respect, have you ever considered counseling to help you be more accepting of Jimmy's disorder? I can see how upset you are. If there is anything going on at home that would account for Jimmy's recent behavioral changes, it's important to inform us. Anyway, I'm sensing that Mom is uncomfortable with our plan. Okay, I will agree to administer even more tests, like the NEPSY, the Rorschach, an adaptive behavior scale and the Thematic Apperception Test. Then we'll see how the results can help us.

Principal: Well, then, it looks like we're out of time.

Parent: But we are not finished here. Can we reschedule another meeting?

Principal: IDEA 2004 encourages schools to have IEP meetings only once a year, so I don't think we can reconvene. But the good news is that per IDEA 2004, we are allowed to make decisions outside the IEP forum. So you and the SPED teacher can meet soon to talk about any unfinished agenda items. Thank you everyone for coming.

****

Principal: Remember, IDEA is not fully funded. We simply don't have the money to provide the service you are requesting for your daughter."

Parent: Our responsibility as a team is to fully comply with the law.

****

Principal: I'm sorry, we have a policy against this.

Parent: What policy is that? Please give me a copy of that policy.
****

Teacher: The law says that.............
Parent: Here is a copy of the law. Please show me where in the law it says.............
****

SPED teacher: The teacher is not trained in special education.
Parent: Inclusion is just good teaching. All teachers should use differentiated instruction to benefit all students. Lets include teacher training in Jimmy's IEP, since this is a service permitted through IDEA.
****

Principal: I cannot expect my teachers to figure out the best way to teach your daughter in every single situation.
Parent: I'm not expecting her to. This is a team effort. That's why there needs to be adequate paid planning time built into the teacher's schedule.
****

Teacher: Your child is not ready to be in the regular classroom all day.
Parent: The law is very clear that my daughter has a right to be in the general education class and it is our responsibility to design the supports and services she needs to be successful. The law is clear that children don't have to earn the right to be in regular education.
****

Principal: Our budget doesn't allow us to buy.............for every student.

Parent: But we're not talking about every student, we are only talking about Sally and her individual needs.

****

We love your daughter and we all want what's best for her.

Parent: What do you mean you love my daughter? You just met her three months ago!

****

SPED teacher: How do you expect your child to learn Math in the general education classroom?

Parent: If you don't know, let's get a consultant to help us figure this out.

****

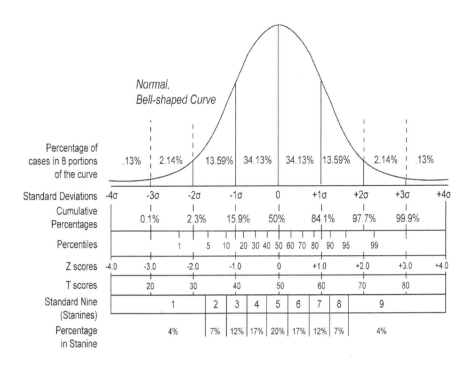

APPENDIX 9 - PSYCHOMETRIC CONVERSION TABLE

Standard Score	Percentile Rank	Scaled Score	ETS Score	T-Score	Z-Score	Description
150	>99.9					Very Superior
149	>99.9					Very Superior
148	99.9					Very Superior
147	99.9					Very Superior
146	99.9					Very Superior
145	99.9	19	800	80	+3.0	Very Superior

144	99.8					Very Superior
143	99.8					Very Superior
142	99.7		775	78	+2.75	Very Superior
141	99.7					Very Superior
140	99.6	18	767	77	+2.67	Very Superior
139	99.5					Very Superior
138	99					Very Superior
137	99		750	75	+2.50	Very Superior

136	99					Very Superior
135	99	17	733	73	+2.33	Very Superior
134	99					Very Superior
133	99		725	72	+2.25	Very Superior
132	98					Very Superior
131	98					Very Superior
130	98	16	700	70	+2.00	Very Superior
129	97					Superior

128	97		675	68	+1.75	Superior
127	96					Superior
126	96					Superior
125	95	15	667	67	+1.67	Superior
124	95					Superior
123	94		650	5	+1.50	Superior
122	93					Superior
121	92					Superior
120	91	14	633	63	+1.33	High Average
119	90					High Average

118	88		325	62	+1.25	High Average
117	87					High Average
116	86					High Average
115	84	13	600	60	+1.00	High Average
114	82					High Average
113	81		575	58	+0.75	High Average
112	79					High Average
111	77					High Average

110	75	12	567	57	+0.67	Average
109	73					Average
108	70		550	55	+0.55	Average
107	68					Average
106	66					Average
105	63	11	533	53	+0.33	Average
104	61					Average
103	58					Average
102	55		525	52	+0.25	Average
101	53					Average
100	50	10	500	50	0.00	Average
99	47					Average

98	45		480	48	-0.25	Average
97	42					Average
96	40					Average
95	37	9	467	47	-0.33	Average
94	34					Average
93	32		450	45	-0.50	Average
92	30					Average
91	27					Average
90	25	8	433	43	-0.67	Average
89	23					Low Average
88	21		425	42	-0.75	Low Average
87	19					Low Average

86	18					Low Average
85	16	7	400	40	-1.00	Low Average
84	14					Low Average
83	13		375	38	-1.75	Low Average
82	12					Low Average
81	10					Low Average
80	9	6	367	37	-1.33	Low Average
79	8					Borderline
78	7		350	35	-1.50	Borderline
77	6					Borderline
76	5					Borderline

75	5	5	333	33	-1.67	Borderline
74	4					Borderline
73	4		325	32	-1.75	Borderline
72	3					Borderline
71	3					Borderline
70	2	4	300	30	-2.00	Borderline
69	2					Impaired
68	2		275	28	-2.25	Impaired
67	1					Mild (69-55)
66	1					Mild (69-55)
65	1	3	267	27	-2.33	Moderate (54-40)

64	1					Moderate (54-40)
63	1		250	25	-2.50	Severe (39-25)
62	1					Severe (39-25)
61	0.5					Profound (<25)
60	0.4	2	233	23	-2.67	Profound (<25)
59	0.3					Profound (<25)
58	0.2		225	22	-2.75	Profound (<25)

57	0.1					Profound (<25)
56	0.1					Profound (<25)
55	0.1	1	200	20	-3.00	Profound (<25)
54	0.1					Profound (<25)
53	0.1					Profound (<25)
52	0.1					Profound (<25)
51	<0.1					Profound (<25)
50	<0.1					Profound (<25)

This is a – compilation of lists Found on Google over the years. Feel free to remind me who to credit! Transition Skills Check List – How Many of These Skills Does the Student still need?

INDEPENDENT LIVING SKILLS
Managing Personal Finances:
- ☐ Count money and make correct change.
- ☐ Manage a savings and checking account.
- ☐ Maintain a personal budget and keep records.
- ☐ Demonstrate personal finance decision-making skills.
- ☐ Make responsible expenditures.
- ☐ Calculate and pay taxes.
- ☐ Use credit responsibly.
- ☐ Pay bills.
- ☐ Deal with renting or leasing.

Nutrition and Fitness:
- ☐ Understand if h/she has food allergies and how to safely deal with them.
- ☐ Understand if I h/she has a specialized diet and how to get medical follow up on his/her dietary needs.
- ☐ Understand the basics of good nutrition, including healthy food choices.
- ☐ Understand funding and budgeting for the purchase of food.
- ☐ Understand the benefits of a health and fitness program.
- ☐ Take part in activities that keep him/her physically fit with modifications as needed.

- ☐ Know and understand the dangers of smoking, drugs, alcohol and abusive behaviors.
- ☐ Know where and how to get help to maintain a healthy lifestyle.
- ☐ Know how to prepare and store food safely.

Raising, Preparing, and Consuming Food:
- ☐ Purchase food and plan meals.
- ☐ Clean food preparation areas.
- ☐ Store food properly.
- ☐ Prepare meals, read labels, and follow recipes.
- ☐ Demonstrate appropriate eating habits.
- ☐ Plan and eat balanced meals.

Overall Domestic Skills:
- ☐ Plan menus
- ☐ Plan and prepare meals.
- ☐ Make shopping list from menu
- ☐ Be safe in kitchen
- ☐ Prepare breakfast, lunch, supper, snack, or pack a lunch
- ☐ Use tools, appliances safely
- ☐ Wash dishes, pots, and pans
- ☐ Clean own room
- ☐ Clean up apartment
- ☐ Do laundry; use washer, dryer, and iron
- ☐ Handle own finances
- ☐ Maintain budget
- ☐ Use time/calendar skills
- ☐ Schedule appointments
- ☐ Perform or arrange for home maintenance.

- ☐ Perform housekeeping tasks.
- ☐ Fill out warranty cards for new appliances and mail them.
- ☐ Fill out warranty cards for new appliances and register it online

Caring for Personal Needs:
- ☐ Exhibit proper grooming and hygiene.
- ☐ Dress appropriately.
- ☐ Obtain health care.
- ☐ Avoid substance abuse.
- ☐ Demonstrate knowledge of common illnesses, prevention and treatment. Maintain physical fitness, nutrition and weight.

Safety Awareness:
- ☐ Identify safety signs.
- ☐ Identify unfamiliar odors.
- ☐ Identify unfamiliar sounds.
- ☐ Demonstrate knowledge and ability to evacuate a building in an emergency. Read and understand basic safety procedures. Obey safety rules when walking during the day or at night.

Recreation and Socialization:
- ☐ Take part in activities with a group of peers/friends.
- ☐ Take part in activities that allow quiet time.
- ☐ Identify activities in the community that are meaningful and participate in them.

Transportation:
- ☐ Know how to use transportation to get from place to place.
- ☐ Know how to get to doctor's office or other appointments.

- [ ] Know who can provide transportation and/or how to make arrangements.
- [ ] Understand safety aspects of walking.
- [ ] Know his/her home address.

Legal and Financial Issues:
- [ ] Know how to apply for Social Security.
- [ ] Know how to apply for food stamps.
- [ ] Know how medical decision making changes at age 18.
- [ ] Know how to manage money.
- [ ] Know how to open a bank account.

Managing Medical Care:
- [ ] Understand his/her medical condition.
- [ ] Have a primary health care provider who knows him/her well and helps him/her in many ways.
- [ ] Know how to take care of his/her medical condition when alone at home.
- [ ] Keep a list of his/her health care providers, their phone numbers and office hours and carry this list in his/her wallet.
- [ ] Have a care plan and understand how to use it in an emergency.
- [ ] Can describe changes/symptoms caused by his/her medical condition.
- [ ] Can call his/her primary care provider when h/she is having problems or needs to give a progress report.
- [ ] Know the difference between an emergency (go to hospital) or illness (call the doctor).
- [ ] Can follow the plan of care recommended by his/her doctor.

Insurance and Care Coordination:

- ☐ Understand that insurance plans may have approved providers.
- ☐ Can identify what services are covered by insurance plans.
- ☐ Know his/her insurance company and how to contact them.
- ☐ Carry his/her insurance card when leaving home or having the info on cellphone
- ☐ Know how and when to get a referral.
- ☐ Know how and when to use insurance and when to pay expenses out of pocket.

Managing Medical Information/Record Keeping:

- ☐ Know how to write down recommendations of the doctor or dentist and have written.
- ☐ Understand follow-up given to him/her or ask for a visit summary.
- ☐ Keep a record of his/her medical information (such as clinic notes, test results, immunizations, summaries, functional assessment, etc.).
- ☐ Know how to keep records organized.
- ☐ Know how to complete a medical records release form, and know when h/she would need to do so.
- ☐ Have a copy of a summary of medical information in a file.
- ☐ Know how to use the Patient Portal from health providers.

Buying and Caring for Clothing:

- ☐ Purchase clothing: Demonstrate knowledge of prices and sales.
- ☐ Iron, mend, wash, and store clothing.
- ☐ Know how to fold clothes and also put them on hangers.

- ☐ Demonstrate use of dry cleaners and laundromat.
- ☐ Check out thrift shops for better prices.

Being a Good Citizen:
- ☐ Demonstrate knowledge of civil rights and responsibilities.
- ☐ Get legal aid.
- ☐ Report a crime.
- ☐ Register with Selective Service at age 18.
- ☐ Demonstrate knowledge of local, state, and federal governments.
- ☐ Demonstrate knowledge of the law and ability to follow the law.
- ☐ Demonstrate knowledge of citizen rights and responsibilities.
- ☐ Vote.

Using Recreational Facilities and Enjoying Leisure Activities:
- ☐ Demonstrate knowledge of available community resources.
- ☐ Choose and plan activities.
- ☐ Demonstrate knowledge of the value of recreation.
- ☐ Engage in group and individual activities.
- ☐ Plan vacation time.
- ☐ Plan a social event.
- ☐ Engage in hobbies, sports, music, arts and crafts.

Getting Around the Community:
- ☐ Differentiate between right side and left side, front and back, to demonstrate location.
- ☐ Demonstrate knowledge of traffic rules and safety. Demonstrate knowledge and use of many means of transportation including carpools.

- ☐ Understand and use a map.
- ☐ Drive a car; obtain a learner's permit, then a driver's license. Obtain car insurance.
- ☐ Download the Uber App and use it.

Community Skills:
- ☐ Make a simple purchase
- ☐ Shop for groceries, clothing
- ☐ Make a phone call
- ☐ Use a cell phone
- ☐ Make necessary appointments
- ☐ Be safe in traffic, cross streets
- ☐ Be safe among strangers
- ☐ Know how to seek help
- ☐ Use vending machines (laundry machines, fare cards, etc.)
- ☐ Order at a fast food restaurant
- ☐ Order at a nice restaurant
- ☐ Handle money
- ☐ Use a bank account
- ☐ Use an ATM
- ☐ Find public restroom
- ☐ Use library
- ☐ Get a haircut
- ☐ Use a cell phone
- ☐ Use a datebook
- ☐ Take prescriptions as directed
- ☐ Use over-the-counter medications appropriately
- ☐ Use sunscreen when needed
- ☐ Use insect repellent when needed.

PERSONAL/SOCIAL SKILLS

- ☐ Identify physical and psychological needs.
- ☐ Identify interests and abilities.
- ☐ Identify emotions.
- ☐ Demonstrate knowledge of physical self.
- ☐ Demonstrate proper care, use, and maintenance of prosthetic devices or sensory aids required. Use appropriate methods to cope with stress.

Feeling Self-Confident:

- ☐ Express feelings of self-worth.
- ☐ Describe others' perception of self.
- ☐ Accept and give praise.
- ☐ Accept and give criticism.
- ☐ Develop confidence in self.
- ☐ Identify and distinguish the proper way to answer and use the telephone.
- ☐ Wear appropriate apparel, using clothes or uniforms to fit social and work situations.

Demonstrating Socially Responsible Behavior:

- ☐ Develop respect for the rights and properties of others.
- ☐ Recognize authority and follow instructions.
- ☐ Demonstrate appropriate behavior and social etiquette in public places and when dating or eating out. Demonstrate knowledge of important character traits. Recognize personal roles.

Demonstrating Good Interpersonal Skills:

- ☐ Demonstrate listening and responding skills.
- ☐ Establish and keep close relationships.

☐ Make and keep friendships.

Demonstrating Independence:

☐ Do things without help.

☐ Accept responsibility for actions.

☐ Get around the community and be able to travel.

☐ Cope with changes in travel schedule.

☐ Cope with being lost.

☐ Follow travel safety procedures.

☐ Choose friends.

☐ Get to school on time.

☐ Decide what to wear.

Demonstrating Personal Problem Solving Skills:

☐ Seek assistance when needed.

☐ Recognize problems.

☐ Anticipate consequences.

☐ Develop and evaluate alternatives.

☐ Develop goals, solutions, and plans.

Good Communication Skills:

☐ Recognize and respond to emergency situations.

☐ Communicate with understanding.

☐ Demonstrate knowledge of social cues and the subtleties of conversation, both verbal and nonverbal. Listen to others.

Social and Personal Skills:

☐ Supply appropriate personal identification

☐ Act appropriately in public

☐ Communicate effectively

☐ Greet people appropriately

☐ "Talk" with friends and co-workers

- ☐ Maintain friendships
- ☐ Be courteous
- ☐ Be responsible
- ☐ Be happy
- ☐ Advocate for self
- ☐ Respect the rights of others
- ☐ Use good grooming, hygiene skills consistently
- ☐ Choose appropriate style of dress, hair, make-up
- ☐ Take prescriptions as directed
- ☐ Use over-the-counter medications appropriately
- ☐ Use sunscreen and insect repellent when needed
- ☐ Use time/calendar skills
- ☐ Seek help when needed

Recreation and Leisure:

- ☐ Use free time for pleasure.
- ☐ Call friends to make plans with them.
- ☐ Choose reasonable activities.
- ☐ Pick a hobby.
- ☐ Perform required activities.
- ☐ Use community resources.
- ☐ Maintain personal fitness.

VOCATIONAL SKILLS

Exploring Occupational Options:

- ☐ Explore occupational possibilities.
- ☐ Identify the rewards of work.
- ☐ Locate sources of occupational and instructional information.
- ☐ Identify personal values met through work.

☐ Identify societal values met through work.

☐ Classify jobs into categories.

☐ Investigate local occupational and instructional opportunities in the community; make site visitations.

☐ Contact the Division of Vocational Rehabilitation (Different names in different states) office and know how to work with them.

☐ Complete an Emergency Information Form (EIF) and given it to all who will need it.

☐ Know his/her rights and responsibilities under the Americans with Disabilities Act (ADA) and the 504 Rehabilitation Act.

☐ Think about possible careers and looked for information about those careers.

☐ Learn about jobs by observing other people (such as family, relatives, and friends) at work and by talking with other adults about what they do for work.

☐ Tour businesses and stores and offices to see what jobs they offer.

☐ Learn about jobs through opportunities offered at school (classes about careers, tests to find out what careers might be best for him/her, job fairs, job program).

☐ Complete a resume and a job application, or know how to do this.

☐ Gain paid or volunteer work experience.

☐ Know how to talk about what h/she needs to be successful in a job.

- ☐ Know how to discuss his/her accommodation needs with an employer.
- ☐ Consider the pros and cons of full-time and part-time work and how these options affect benefits offered.

Job Search:
- ☐ Look for jobs (advertisements in the newspaper and online, neighborhood help-wanted signs, and local resources).
- ☐ Fill out job applications.
- ☐ Apply for jobs online.
- ☐ Write résumés and cover letters.
- ☐ Apply for a job.
- ☐ Obtain necessary identification (photo ID, birth certificate).
- ☐ Fill out paperwork (W2 forms, I-9 forms, employer paperwork).
- ☐ Having interviewing skills.

Selecting and Planning Occupational Choices:
- ☐ Make realistic occupational choices.
- ☐ Identify requirements of appropriate and available jobs.
- ☐ Identify occupational aptitudes.
- ☐ Identify main occupational interests.
- ☐ Identify major occupational needs.

Appropriate Work Habits and Behavior:
- ☐ Follow directions and observe regulations.
- ☐ Recognize the importance of attendance and punctuality.
- ☐ Recognize the importance of supervision.
- ☐ Demonstrate knowledge of safety.
- ☐ Work with others.
- ☐ Meet demands for high-quality work.

- ☐ Work at a satisfactory rate.
- ☐ Demonstrate knowledge of competitive standards.
- ☐ Know how to adjust to changes in employment.

Sufficient Physical and Manual Skills:
- ☐ Demonstrate stamina and endurance.
- ☐ Demonstrate satisfactory balance and coordination.
- ☐ Demonstrate manual dexterity.
- ☐ Demonstrate sensory discrimination.

Obtaining Specific Occupational Skills:
- ☐ Attend pre-vocational learning stations or centers.
- ☐ Take advantage of in-school work experiences.
- ☐ Take advantage of volunteer experiences.
- ☐ Serve in community rotations.
- ☐ Take advantage of work/study services.
- ☐ Attend vocational classrooms.
- ☐ Obtain special vocational education.
- ☐ Obtain on-the-job training.

Vocational Skills on the Job
- ☐ Use a time card and punch clock.
- ☐ Arrive to work on time.
- ☐ Call when sick.
- ☐ Request vacation time.
- ☐ Use the appropriate voice tone and volume when speaking.
- ☐ Accept instructions and corrections.
- ☐ Know appropriate interaction with coworkers (i.e., getting along; social problem solving; making friends; and recognizing personal, professional, and sexual boundaries).
- ☐ Follow directions.

- [ ] Accept supervision.
- [ ] Get to and from work, on time.
- [ ] Perform work satisfactorily.
- [ ] Work cooperatively with others.
- [ ] Take break or lunch appropriately.
- [ ] Wear suitable clothing.
- [ ] Use appropriate safety procedures.

Social and Interpersonal Skills on the Job

- [ ] Answer the phone and taking a message.
- [ ] Make necessary phone calls to employers and other professionals as part of a job requirement.
- [ ] Display appropriate workplace behavior and etiquette.
- [ ] Know appropriate topics for discussion in the workplace.
- [ ] Know when and when not to socialize on the job.
- [ ] Learn how to protect yourself from victimization.
- [ ] Learn social problem-solving techniques.

PREPARED FOR COLLEGE OR POSTSECONDARY OPTIONS

- [ ] Testing is updated.
- [ ] Student possesses copies of testing.
- [ ] Student knows how to safely maintain files of previous testing, including storing it electronically.
- [ ] Student has a record of a diagnosis from his/her treating physician, which includes information about how the disability affects the student.
- [ ] Student has an appropriate transition plan and is receiving transition services to prepare him/her to attend college or a postsecondary option.
- [ ] Knowledge of study skills is adequate.

- ☐ Student understands his/her disability.
- ☐ Student understands and can articulate how much support h/she needs.
- ☐ Student understands and can articulate what kind of support h/she needs.
- ☐ Student understands and can articulate his/her strengths and weaknesses and also what compensating techniques and accommodations are effective.
- ☐ Student understands how his/her disability is connected to social experiences with peers, family, teachers, and employers.
- ☐ Student can advocate for his/her needs.
- ☐ Student accepts responsibility for their own success.
- ☐ Student has completed the appropriate preparatory curriculum.
- ☐ Student has completed any supplemental postsecondary education preparatory programs needed for succeed at college.
- ☐ Student has good computer skills.
- ☐ Student has given thought as to whether or not h/she should disclose his/her disability when applying for college.
- ☐ A vocational assessment was completed to clarify present and future goals.
- ☐ Student has the independent living skills needed to live on campus.
- ☐ Student has good time management skills.
- ☐ Student understands his/her rights under Section 504 of the Rehabilitation Act of 1973 and the ADA.

- ☐ Student has information on special exam arrangements for SAT and/or ACT.
- ☐ Student knows how to request accommodations for testing, including extended time on tests, alternative testing formats, etc.
- ☐ Student has contacted the Disability Service Offices of colleges before applying (if appropriate).
- ☐ Student has received information on what services and support are available and the process for accessing accommodations at school.
- ☐ Student understands what are academic adjustments and auxiliary aids and services (see Section 504 regulations at 34 C.F.R. § 104.44(a)).
- ☐ Student has visited colleges before making a choice.
- ☐ Student has skills to get involved on campus.
- ☐ Student has made his/her own decision to attend college or other postsecondary program.

Amy R. Smith
55 Witten Drive   Stamfire, CT 06906
Home: 203-123-4567   cell: 203-891-2345
AmySmith@ail.com

May 17, 2016

Nelly Koch, Special Education Teacher
Happy Elementary School
345 Main Street
Stamfire, CT 06906

Re: Request for reading evaluation for Jimmy Smith / Faxed and also send via first class mail

Dear Nelly,

My son Jimmy Smith is a 10 year old boy in the 5th grade, yet he reads on a kindergarten level and has made minimal progress during his 7 years at Happy Elementary School. Despite his significant challenges, he has never had a formal reading evaluation nor has he had services from a reading specialist in Stamfire Public Schools.

What is the plan to bring Jimmy's reading ability to grade level?

I am requesting a comprehensive reading evaluation by a qualified reading specialist to determine what peer-reviewed, evidence-based reading program Jimmy needs to become a proficient reader. In order to avoid any misunderstanding as to what exactly I am asking for, I have attached a list of reading definitions from No Child Left Behind. Given the enormous reading gap between Jimmy and his same-age peers, I am asking that this request be attended to without any delay.

Thank you.

Amy R. Smith

Copy to: Molly Arbet, Principal of Happy Elementary School
Sally Simpson, 5th grade teacher, Happy Elementary School

Enclosure: 4 Definitions About Reading from No Child Left Behind

4 Definitions About Reading from No Child Left Behind

1. Legal definition of reading The term 'reading' means a complex system of deriving meaning from print that requires all of the following:

(A) The skills and knowledge to understand how phonemes, or speech sounds, are connected to print.

(B) The ability to decode unfamiliar words.

(C) The ability to read fluently.

(D) Sufficient background information and vocabulary to foster reading comprehension.

(E) The development of appropriate active strategies to construct meaning from print.

(F) The development and maintenance of a motivation to read.

2. Legal definition of the essential components of reading instruction

The term 'essential components of reading instruction' means explicit and systematic instruction in-

(A) phonemic awareness;

(B) phonics;

(C) vocabulary development;

(D) reading fluency, including oral reading skills; and

(E) reading comprehension strategies.

3. Legal definition of scientifically based reading research

The term 'scientifically based reading research' means research that-

(A) applies rigorous, systematic, and objective procedures to obtain valid knowledge relevant to reading development, reading instruction, and reading difficulties; and

(B) includes research that-

(i) employs systematic, empirical methods that draw on observation or experiment;

(ii) involves rigorous data analyses that are adequate to test the stated hypotheses and justify the general conclusions drawn;

(iii) relies on measurements or observational methods that provide valid data across evaluators and observers and across multiple measurements and
observations; and

(iv) has been accepted by a peer-reviewed journal or approved by a panel of independent experts through a comparably rigorous, objective, and scientific review.

4. Legal definition of a diagnostic reading assessment The term 'diagnostic reading assessment' means an assessment that is-

(i) valid, reliable, and based on scientifically based reading research; and

(ii) used for the purpose of-

(I) identifying a child's specific areas of strengths and weaknesses so that the child has learned to read by the end of grade 3;

(II) determining any difficulties that a child may have in learning to read and the potential cause of such difficulties; and

(III) helping to determine possible reading intervention strategies and related special needs.

APPENDIX 12 - UNDERSTANDING THE NRP FIVE CRITICAL AREAS THAT EFFECTIVE READING INSTRUCTION MUST ADDRESS

The National Reading Panel identified five critical areas that effective reading instruction must address. You MUST understand the five components of reading! They are pasted below. Thanks to Sheryl Knapp, M.ED., A/AOGPE. Meet Sheryl at http://www.literacylearningct.com

1. Phonemic Awareness: the ability to hear & manipulate sounds in words.
•   Phonemes are the smallest units of sound in a spoken language. Phonemic awareness falls on a continuum of phonological awareness tasks – ranging from rhyming to blending, segmenting, and otherwise identifying and manipulating sounds (or phonemes) within words. These latter, more advanced skills, referred to as phonemic awareness, are critical to learning to read and spell.
•   While many children who read – or are read to – at home and school frequently acquire phonemic awareness without being taught it explicitly, those with disabilities frequently require explicit instruction in breaking apart words into component sounds, and blending these sounds to form syllables and words. These are skills that ideally should be acquired by kindergarten or the first grade, and typically require about 20 hours of dedicated instruction on average – but it tends to be an area of particular difficulty for students with dyslexia, and those students with intellectual disabilities.
•   However, phonemic (or phonological) awareness instruction should be viewed as a means to an end, not an end itself; it is part of an overall reading intervention – not the entire intervention. Students with intellectual disabilities frequently struggle with rhyming tasks in particular, but it is important not to stall instruction to work on this (or any other PA task) for an extended period of time, especially for older students.
•   Phonemic awareness tasks include:
    •   Sound isolation: What is the first sound in 'rose'? What is the last sound in 'back'?

- Phoneme deletion: What word would be left if the /p/ sound were taken away from spit? (sit)
- Word to word matching: Do pen and pipe begin with the same sound?
- Blending: What word would we have if we put these sounds together: /ch/, /a/, /t/?
- Segmentation: Tell me the sounds in 'truck' (/t/ /r/ /u/ /k/).
- Phoneme counting: How many sounds do you hear in the word 'cake'?
- Phoneme deletion: Odd word out: Which word starts with a different sound: bag, nine, beach, bike?
- Sound to word matching: Is there a /k/ sound in 'bike'? What sound do you hear in 'meat' that is missing in 'eat'?

2. Phonics: the relationship between letters and their associated sounds.

- There is a predictable relationship between phonemes (the sounds in spoken language) and graphemes, the letters that represent those sounds in written language, and this information can be used to read or decode ("sound out") words. This is also known as the Alphabetic Principle. Mastery of these "rules" is necessary in order to become a proficient reader or speller and does not require high level cognitive processes; decoding ability tends to be independent of IQ, making it achievable for many if not most students with intellectual disabilities. Interestingly, struggling readers with ID tend to make the greatest gains on average from systematic phonetic instruction.

- Systematic and explicit phonics instruction should teach decoding (reading) and encoding (spelling) concurrently, as they tend to be inverse tasks: reading involves translating letters into sounds, and spelling translating sounds into letters. It is critical that this instruction maintains the fidelity of the underlying methodology (e.g., Orton-Gillingham) or program (Wilson Reading System®, S.P.I.R.E., SeeingStars®, etc.), and encompasses:

  - Explicit instruction in sound-symbol correspondences;
  - Word analysis, from reading and spelling perspectives; and
  - Reading and spelling words within connected text (sentences and passages), providing the opportunity to practice applying phonetic concepts.

- Although phonetic instruction tends to be most effective when introduced early (in kindergarten or 1st grade), recent research on the Wilson Reading System® shows equivalent gains for older students.

- Methodologies to avoid include:
  - Literature based programs that emphasize reading and writing activities;
  - Basal reading programs that focus on whole words and do not specifically teach children how to blend letters to pronounce words; and
  - Sight word programs (e.g. Edmark), which also do not explicitly teach critical phonetic concepts.

3.   Fluency: the ability to read accurately, fluidly, & with appropriate prosody (phrasing and inflection).

- "Because fluent readers do not have to concentrate on decoding words, they can focus their attention on what the text means." (National Institute for Literacy, 2002).

- The ability to read text accurately and fluidly, with appropriate inflection and pace, is critical to comprehension. Fluent readers have learned to recognize printed words automatically, without requiring the use of significant cognitive resources, freeing up these critical resources for use in the application of specific comprehension strategies such as drawing inferences. Yet the NAEP – our Nation's "report card" – found that 44% of fourth graders exhibit poor reading fluency.

- Although reading fluency can, for some students, improve through repeated oral reading activities (provided that ongoing feedback is provided), such interventions do not take the place of explicit, sequential, evidence-based phonetic instruction. Most dysfluent readers lack automaticity with the application of required phonetic concepts, and therefore require this instruction in order to achieve fluency. It is important to add that sustained silent reading has not been shown to improve fluency.

- Progress with regard to reading rate can easily be charted, although they typically utilize grade-level text which can provide misleading data for students receiving phonetic instruction; frequently, a student's reading rate temporarily increases when s/he is taught to "sound out" words rather than read by sight, which tends to be a quicker process for students who are not yet automatic with the application of phonetic concepts. Standardized measures of reading fluency include the Dynamic Indicators of Basic Early Literacy Skills (DIBELS) and AIMSWeb®.

4. Vocabulary: the ability to recognize printed and orally presented words, and to convey that meaning.

•   Vocabulary encompasses both receptive (what an individual knows) and expressive (what s/he can express) domains. Receptive vocabulary has been found to have a far greater impact on reading acquisition than does expressive vocabulary; put another way, what is most important is that students know the meaning of words, as opposed to possessing the ability to convey this knowledge. This is especially important for students with more pervasive disabilities who frequently have relatively strong receptive skills.

•   Vocabulary is an important factor in reading comprehension, as readers cannot understand what they are reading unless they know what most of the words mean. Not surprisingly, comprehension improves as a student's vocabulary grows.

•   There is not a lot of good research regarding the best way to build vocabulary, but we do know that:

   •   Vocabulary is learned both indirectly, through everyday experiences (e.g., conversations with adults, reading and being read to, etc.), and directly, through explicit instruction in both individual words and word-learning strategies (such as using context to derive the meaning of an unknown word).

   •   The best way to build vocabulary is by reading – or being read to. Printed text possesses a higher standard of language/vocabulary than oral language, exposing students to novel words they are less likely to hear in spontaneous language. Unfortunately, poor readers tend to read less – which, in turn, causes them to fall further behind due to the impact on vocabulary.

   •   Pre-teaching specific words before reading text helps both vocabulary acquisition and reading comprehension.

   •   The traditional way of introducing vocabulary – by giving students lists of words to memorize weekly – does not result in sustainable vocabulary gains. Students must use words repeatedly – and have repeated exposure to them – in order to gain "ownership" of them.

   •   Morphological instruction – or instruction in breaking words into meaningful units (prefixes, suffixes, and roots) and analyzing the meaning of each part – also produces sustainable vocabulary gains. If a student learns the meaning of the root word port (to carry), for instance, as well as several associated prefixes (trans, im, re, de, etc.) and suffixes (tion, ee, ed, etc.), s/he can use this information to derive the meaning of numerous words.

- Unfortunately, poor readers tend to read less, which in turn weakens their vocabulary relative to peers – making them fall even further behind (and increasing their distaste for reading, which compounds the gap). This is known as the "Matthew Effect": poor readers become even poorer readers relative to peers due to the effects of their initial struggles with reading.

5. Text Comprehension: the ability to understand (and access content from) text.

- Reading comprehension – or the ability to engage with and obtain content and meaning from text – is the ultimate purpose for reading. If readers can read the words but do not understand what they are reading, they are not really "reading". Instruction in comprehension can help students understand what they read, remember what they read, and communicate with others about what they read.

- The ability to access content from printed text is the culmination of many factors; if any of these component skills (decoding or word identification, vocabulary, prior knowledge of the content, and especially reading fluency), then comprehension will also likely be impaired – making it look as if the student's struggles are rooted in the comprehension process as opposed to these underlying skills.

- Effective comprehension instruction utilizes a variety of teaching strategies – including direct instruction/explanation, teacher modeling, guided practice, and application – in order to systematically teach the following comprehension strategies in particular:

    a) Determining what information is most (and least) important;
    b) Synthesizing or summarizing content to derive the central theme or "big picture";
    c) Making inferences – or reaching conclusions that are not explicitly stated in the text;
    d) Visualizing text as students are reading (or hearing) it;

e) Monitoring comprehension, checking that the text makes sense as it is being read;

f) Continually engaging with the text, generating questions and opinions; and

g) Using prior knowledge to enhance (and not impede) understanding.

Gebser Notice Template

1. In writing, address the notification to a specific person and date the letter.

2. Write the letter to a person who has the authority to investigate and the authority to correct the wrong.

3. Note that the school district is a recipient of federal financial assistance.

4. State the past or continuing discriminatory activity against your child.

5. State that the school district has control over both the site of the discrimination and over any school personnel involved.

6. Explain that the discrimination was not a single act but was severe and pervasive.

7. Tell how the discrimination excluded your child from continued participation in school or denied your child the benefits to which other students in school have access.

8. Explain, as well as you can, what you would like the school to do to stop the discrimination or to remediate the harm the discrimination has done to your child.

9. Ask for a copy of a school district grievance procedure under Section 504 (even if your child has an IEP under IDEA). Not having this information may result in continued discrimination.

10. State that if the person receiving this letter does not investigate or does not take effective corrective action, that you may claim that the district showed deliberate indifference to the discrimination. You may also want to add a date you expect to hear back from the district in regards to your letter.

These steps are adapted from the late attorney Reed Martin's "10 steps to making a successful complaint.

Law Office of Anne I. Treimanis, LLC
161 East Avenue, Suite 104
Norwalk, CT 06851
203-838-5485 Fax 203-838-4222
attorneytreimanis@gmail.com http://.spedlawyers.com

February 21, 2016

Jackie Smith, Esq.
Connecticut State Department of Education
Bureau of Special Education
Due Process Unit
P.O. Box 2219, Room 359
Hartford, CT 06145-2219

Re: Request for Public Records from the Connecticut State Department of Education

Dear Attorney Smith,

I am writing today because I would like additional information related to the operations, policies and procedures of the Connecticut State Department of Education concerning special education. I am asking for this information under the Freedom of Information Act.

Connecticut's Freedom of Information Act is designed to ensure citizen access to the records and meetings of public agencies in the State of Connecticut. This request reasonably describes identifiable records or information and I believe no express provision of law exists exempting the requested records from disclosure. Should the Connecticut State Department of Education, Bureau of Special Education find any portion of any requested record exempt from release due to concerns related to disclosure of personally identifiable student information, I ask that you redact the personally identifiable information to alleviate any confidentiality concerns. I am requesting the right to review and inspect the following records:

• All Complaints with full files filed against School Districts and educational agencies using the Connecticut Complaint Resolution Process from the beginning of time until the date of this request.

As you know, The Individuals with Disabilities Education Act (IDEA 2004) establishes the requirement that State Education Agencies adopt written procedures for the investigation and resolution of any complaint which alleges that an education agency has violated a requirement of the IDEA. My request includes:

1. The written procedures that the CT State Department of Education has adopted to investigate and resolve any complaint that that alleges that an education agency has violated a requirement of the IDEA.
2. A copy of each and every complaint that has been filed in writing with the CT State Department of Education which alleges that an education agency has violated a requirement of the IDEA.
3. A copy of the education agency's response to the complaint.
4. A copy of the resolution of the complaint.

If you decide to withhold any portion of any record requested, I ask that you provide a list identifying what you have withheld. I ask that you cite specific exemption(s) being relied upon to withhold information. I also ask that you make available for inspection any records that indicate, suggest, or otherwise identify the prior existence of other records related to the request that may have been modified or destroyed.

There is a public interest in the requested records, and they are not being requested for commercial purpose. I seek this information because it edifies the operations and activities of Connecticut school districts, education agencies that serve students in Connecticut, and the Connecticut State Department of Education. This is an important issue for the public and public interest clearly outweighs all other interests. The public interest is served by the full and timely disclosure of all requested records.

This information can be scanned to me on pdf files and does not need to be photocopied. I will gladly provide the district with a thumb drive, if you choose this route.

I can also accept the records via drop box or you can post the information on your website.

Please respond to this request in a reasonable time period. If the records I am requesting take longer than 10 business days to produce, please contact me with information about when I can expect access to review and inspect the requested records. If there are any fees associated with this request, I ask that you inform me ahead of time.

Very truly yours,

Attorney Anne Treimanis

Copy: Bureau Chief of Special Education

Nora Belanger, Esq. http://www.norabelangerlaw.com

Gerri Fleming, The Advocacy Office of Gerri Fleming, LLC
http://www.ctadvocacy.com

Sheryl Knapp, M.ED., A/AOGPE http://www.literacylearningct.com

Colleen Tomko http://www.kidstogether.org. Please shop for her disability-themed gifts at http://www.cafepress.com/theparentside

Kathleen Whitbread, Ph.D http://kathleenwhitbread.com and https://openbooksopendoors.com

Peter Wright, Esq. and Pamela Darr Wright, MA, MSW
http://www.wrightslaw.com – Pete and Pam are rock stars in this field. It's pretty much impossible to write a book on special education strategies without seeing reflections of what this dynamic duo has taught us!

Do you want to see your name here? Send your tips or sample forms to do.not.tweet.tips@gmail.com. If we use your tips or forms in the next edition of this book, we will credit you.

I Have a Dream

By Anne I. Treimanis, Esq,

Liberally adapted from the "I Have a Dream" speech, one of the world's most acclaimed speeches ever written, by the great Dr. Martin Luther King, Jr.

I am happy to share this book with you today in what will go down in history as the greatest tips on surviving special education in the history of our nation.

Two score years ago, a great American Congress, in whose shadow we still stand today, signed the Education of All Handicapped Children's Act, Now known as IDEA, the Individuals With Disabilities Education Act. This momentous decree came as a great beacon light of hope to millions of children with disabilities who had been seared in the flames of withering injustice. It came as a joyous daybreak to end the long night of their captivity. 1.75 million children with disabilities received no educational services at all, and 2.5 million children with disabilities were receiving an inappropriate education.

But forty years later, the students with disabilities still do not receive FAPE. Forty years later, the life of the students with disabilities is still sadly crippled by the manacles of segregation and the chains of discrimination. Forty years later, the students with disabilities lives on a lonely island of segregation, and waste their time in inappropriate programs. Forty years later, the students with disabilities is still languishing in the corners of American society, many illiterate, many unemployed, and finds himself an exile in his own land. So we have come here today to dramatize a shameful condition.

In a sense we have come to our nation's capital to cash a check. This note was a promise that all students with disabilities would be guaranteed the unalienable rights of FAPE, LRE, meaningful participation in the IEP programs, appropriate evaluations, and IEPs where the I truly stands for individualized.

It is obvious today that America has defaulted on this promissory note insofar as her citizens with disabilities are concerned. Instead of honoring this sacred obligation, America has given the students with disabilities a bad check, a check which has come back marked "insufficient funds." But we refuse to believe that the schools are bankrupt. Now is the time to make real the promises of the Individuals with Disabilities Education Act.

It would be fatal for the nation to overlook the urgency of the moment. This sweltering summer of the students with disabilities' legitimate discontent will not pass until there is an invigorating autumn of freedom and equality. Two-thousand-sixteen is not an end, but a beginning. Those who hope that the students with disabilities needed to blow off steam and will now be content will have a rude awakening if the nation returns to business as usual. There will be neither rest nor tranquility in America until the students with disabilities are granted their federal rights.

We must learn how to use effective strategies when advocating for our children. Parents must sit as meaningful participants at the IEP, we must not be afraid to exercise our procedural safeguards. The marvelous new militancy which has engulfed the Disability Community must not lead us to a distrust of all school districts, for many of our educators, as evidenced by their presence in the schools, have come to realize that their destiny is tied up with our destiny. They have come to realize that their freedom is inextricably bound to our freedom. We cannot walk alone.

There are those who are asking the devotees of civil rights, "When will you be satisfied?" We can never be satisfied as long as the students with disabilities are second class citizens. We can never be satisfied, as long as students with intellectual disabilities are not given evidence-based reading programs. We cannot be satisfied as long as the students with disabilities are suspended for behaviors which are manifestations of their disabilities. We can never be satisfied as long as our children are unnecessarily restrained, secluded, and in Georgia, little boys are paddled. We cannot be satisfied as long as students with a disability are given calculators instead of being taught math. No, no, we are not satisfied, and we will not be satisfied until students with IEPs receive FAPE.

I have a dream that each student receiving special education services will have an IEP which will confer meaningful educational benefit.

I have a dream that that evaluations of children are technically sound, nondiscriminatory, and effective in gathering the information needed to determine if the child has a disability and the nature and extent of the special education and related services that the child needs.

I have a dream that we embrace the findings of our Congress who said that *almost 30 years of research and experience has demonstrated that the education of children with disabilities can be made more effective by having high expectations for such children and ensuring their access to the general education curriculum in the regular classroom, to the maximum extent possible.*

I have a dream that we embrace the findings of our Congress who said that *Disability is a natural part of the human experience and in no way diminishes the right of individuals to participate in, or contribute to, society. And that improving educational results for children with disabilities is an essential element of our national policy of ensuring equality of opportunity, full participation, independent living, and economic self-sufficiency for individuals with disabilities.*

I have a dream that students will be involved in developing their own IEPs.

And if America is to be a great nation this must become true. So let freedom ring from the Los Angeles Unified School District of California to the New York City Board of Education!

And when this happens, when we allow freedom to ring, we will be able to speed up that day when all of God's children, with and without disabilities, their families, and the schools, will be able to join hands and sing in the words of the IDEA regulations, "FAPE at last! FAPE at last! thank God Almighty, we have FAPE at last!"

Made in the USA
Columbia, SC
04 February 2019